The Grace *Awakening* Devotional

A Thirty-Day Walk in the Freedom of Grace

MINIBOOKS

Abraham: A Model of Pioneer Faith

David: A Model of Pioneer Courage

Esther: A Model of Pioneer
Independence

Moses: A Model of Pioneer Vision

Nehemiah: A Model of Pioneer
Determination

BOOKLETS

Anger

Attitudes

Commitment

Dealing with Defiance

Demonism

Destiny

Divorce

Eternal Security

Forgiving and Forgetting

Fun Is Contagious!

God's Will

Hope

Impossibilities

Integrity

Intimacy with the Almighty

Leisure

The Lonely Whine of the Top Dog

Make Your Dream Come True

Making the Weak Family Strong

Moral Purity

Our Mediator

Peace . . . in Spite of Panic

Portrait of a Faithful Father

The Power of a Promise

Prayer

Reflections from the Heart—
A Prayer Journal

Seeking the Shepherd's Heart—
A Prayer Journal

Sensuality

Stress

This is No Time for Wimps

Tongues

When Your Comfort Zone Gets
the Squeeze

Woman

BOOKS FOR CHILDREN

Paw Paw Chuck's Big Ideas in the Bible

CHARLES R. SWINDOLL

The Grace *Awakening* Devotional

A Thirty-Day Walk in the Freedom of Grace

W PUBLISHING GROUP™

www.wpublishinggroup.com

A Division of Thomas Nelson, Inc.
www.ThomasNelson.com

Published by W Publishing Group, a division of Thomas Nelson, Inc., P. O. Box 141000, Nashville, TN 37214.

Unless otherwise indicated, Scripture quotations used in this book are from the New American Standard Bible (NASB) © 1960, 1962, 1963, 1968, 1971, 1972, 1973, 1975, 1977, 1995 by The Lockman Foundation. Used by permission.

Scripture quotations marked MSG are taken from The Message. Copyright © 1993, 1994, 1995, 1996, 2000, 2001, 2001. Used by permission of NavPress Publishing Group.

Scripture quotations marked NIV are taken from the Holy Bible, New International Version. Copyright © 1973, 1978, 1984, by the International Bible Society. Used by permission of Zondervan Bible Publishers.

Scripture quotations marked NKJV are taken from the New King James Version. Copyright © 1979, 1980, 1982, Thomas Nelson, Inc., Publisher.

Scripture quotations marked NLT are taken from the Holy Bible, New Living Translation, copyright © 1996. Used by permission of Tyndale House Publishers, Inc., Wheaton, Illinois 60189. All rights reserved.

Produced with the assistance of The Livingstone Corporation: (www.LivingstoneCorporation.com). Project staff includes Katherine Cloyd, Neil Wilson, Linda Taylor, and Dave Veerman.

Library of Congress Catloging-in-Publication Data:

Swindoll, Charles R. The grace awakening: 30-day devotional readings / by Charles R. Swindoll.
p. cm.

ISBN 0-8499-4440-6

1. Grace (Theology) 2. Devotional calendars. I. Title.
BT761.3.S95   2003
234–dc22   2003015622
                                                                        CIP

Printed in the United States of America
03 04 05 06 07 BVG 9 8 7 6 5 4 3 2 1

 CONTENTS

Contents

 PREFACE

When *The Grace Awakening* first appeared in 1990, Chuck Swindoll had wanted to address what he perceived as "grace killers," people who restrain and limit the dynamic potential of the Christian life. Among the most visible and vicious are those who criticize, condemn, and crush believers' hopes of joyful living. Chuck warned that legalism in the church—hiding behind the mask of orthodoxy or piety—was stealing the happiness of believers and holding faith hostage. What we needed at that hour was awakening.

Within days of the book's release, the responses began flooding in. Letters, cards, and reviews came from grateful pastors, teachers, and other Christians all over the country. The book has found a steady audience for more than a decade. Certain themes have emerged from the responses down through the years. Some correspondents said they had often felt imprisoned in their faith until they recognized their own need for a "grace awakening." Suddenly they understood the reality of the regeneration that Christ

had meant for His followers to enjoy. "If we are new crea-
tures in Christ," they asked, "why aren't we rejoicing more
and worrying less?" At the other end of the spectrum, however, came sad correspondence from some Christian leaders who reported that they had lost the battle with their
churches or organizations, had become weary of the
assaults, and had resigned from their positions. They had
been awakened, but they couldn't awaken anyone else! All
these letter writers expressed in one way or another a
hunger to be reconnected with grace in an unencum-
bered way. And all reported their gratitude over the help
they received in the pages of *The Grace Awakening*.

Since the release of the book, the world has continued
its dramatic changes. In addition to the political changes
in Europe, the Middle East, and Asia, there have been
startling moral and ethical revolutions as well—an awakening of conscience and character of amazing propor-
tions. Christianity has been breaking out around the
world. Heightened tensions over terrorism and radical dis-
tortions of other religions have highlighted the need for
Christians to be clear and compelling in sharing the
gospel of grace, holding to the truth of Scripture and freedom in Christ.

Paul writes in Romans 12:6 that "since we have gifts
that differ according to the grace given to us, each of us is
to exercise them accordingly." Indeed, each one of us has

gifts, but it is the hope of the reflections in this devotional, as well as the book on which they are based, that we should become a generation of believers molded into the image of Christ, walking boldly in the freedom of faith that our Lord intended. For when that occurs, *The Grace Awakening* is not simply a book worth reading, but a life worth living.

—THE PUBLISHER

 INTRODUCTION

*A*new movement is on the horizon. It is a movement of freedom, a joyful release from the things that have bound us far too long. More and more Christians are realizing that the man-made restrictions and legalistic regulations under which they have been living have not come from the God of grace but have been enforced by people who do not want others to be free. It is not an overstatement to describe this movement as an awakening that is beginning to sweep across the country. Nothing could please me more. This awakening to freedom is long overdue. It fits the times in which we are living.

When the sixteenth-century European Reformers brandished the torch of freedom and stood against the religious legalists of their era, grace was the battle cry: salvation by grace alone, a walk of faith without fear of eternal damnation. The church hated them and called them heretics. When the eighteenth- and early nineteenth-century revival, preached fervently by John Wesley, Jonathan Edwards, George Whitefield, and a handful of other risk-taking spokesmen for God spread across Great Britain and into America, it was again grace that led the way. And there was again strong resistance from those who frowned upon their message of freedom in Christ. Interestingly, that sweeping movement came to be known as "The Great Awakening." What I am sensing these days is yet another awakening in the genre of those history-making movements. Perhaps it is best defined as "The Grace Awakening," a message whose time has come.

For the next thirty days, I trust you will experience a liberating dose of God's grace. I also trust it will leave you hungry to know and experience more, for grace keeps us fully engaged with God, who is the inexhaustible source of grace. Once you've experienced a grace awakening, you will be awake in new ways to all God wants to do in your life.

—CHARLES SWINDOLL

DAY 1

Dear brothers and sisters, if another Christian is overcome by some sin, you who are godly should gently and humbly help that person back onto the right path. And be careful not to fall into the same temptation yourself.

Galatians 6:1 NLT

CLAIMING THE PACKAGE

*T*his day—this very moment—millions are living their lives in shame, fear, and intimidation who should be free, productive individuals. The tragedy is they think it is the way they should be. They have never known the truth that could set them free. They are victimized, existing as if living on death row instead of enjoying the beauty and fresh air of the abundant life Christ modeled and made possible for all of His followers to claim. Unfortunately, most don't have a clue as to what they are missing.

That whole package, in a word, is *grace*. That's what is being assaulted so continually, so violently. Those who aren't comfortable denying it have decided to debate it. Similar to the days of the Protestant Reformation, grace has again become a theological football kicked from one end of the field to the other as theologians and preachers, scholars and students argue over terms like frustrated coaches on opposite sides trying to gain advantage over each other. It is a classic no-win debate that trivializes the issue and leaves the masses who watch the fight from the stands confused, polarized, or worst of all, bored. Grace was meant to be received and lived out to the fullest, not dissected and analyzed by those who would rather argue than eat. Enough of this! It's time for grace to be awakened and released, not denied . . . to be enjoyed and freely given, not debated.

Grace received but unexpressed is dead grace. To spend one's time debating how grace is received or how much commitment is necessary for salvation, without getting into what it means to live by grace and enjoy the magnificent freedom it provides, quickly leads to a counterproductive argument. It becomes little more than another tedious trivial pursuit where the majority of God's people spend days looking back and asking, "How did we receive it?" instead of looking ahead and announcing, "Grace is ours . . . let's live it!" Deny it or debate it and we kill it. My plea is that we claim it and allow it to set us free. When we do, grace will become what it was meant to *be—really* amazing! When that happens, our whole countenance changes.

🌿 REFLECTING ON GRACE

If you know any believers (even yourself) who are "living their lives in shame, fear, and intimidation," describe what you think has caused those feelings.

How would you define God's grace?

In what ways has your life been most deeply affected by God's grace?

🌿 AWAKENING TO GRACE

John 8:3–11

The scribes and the Pharisees brought a woman caught in adultery, and having set her in the center of the court, they said to Him, "Teacher, this woman has been caught in adultery, in the very act. Now in the Law Moses commanded us to stone such women; what then do You say?" And they were saying this, testing Him, so that they might have grounds for accusing Him. But

> *Jesus stooped down and with His finger wrote on the ground. But when they persisted in asking Him, He straightened up, and said to them, "He who is without sin among you, let him be the first to throw a stone at her." And again He stooped down and wrote on the ground. When they heard it, they began to go out one by one, beginning with the older ones, and He was left alone, and the woman, where she was, in the center of the court. Straightening up, Jesus said to her, "Woman, where are they? Did no one condemn you?" She said, "No one, Lord." And Jesus said, "Neither do I condemn you. Go. From now on sin no more."*

According to John, the gospel writer, what was the real issue for the scribes and Pharisees when they asked Jesus to determine the fate of this woman?

How did Jesus express grace toward the woman, without letting her off the hook for her behavior or condoning her sin?

How did Jesus express grace toward the woman's accusers?

WALKING IN GRACE

What does it mean to you to be able to enjoy "the beauty and fresh air of the abundant life" Christ has given you?

"Grace is ours . . . let's live it!" How will you live God's grace today?

Is this approach to grace different than the way you were raised? If so, how?

DAY 2

In Him we have redemption through His blood, the forgiveness of our trespasses, according to the riches of His grace.

Ephesians 1:7

THE POWER OF GRACE

Candidly, I know of nothing that has the power to change us from within like the freedom that comes through grace. It's so amazing it will change not only our hearts but also our faces. And goodness knows, some of us are overdue for a face change! Were you reared by parents whose faces said "No"? Or are you married to someone with a "No" face? If that is true, you envy those who had "Yes"-face parents or are married to "Yes"-face mates. All of us are drawn to those whose faces invite us in and urge us on.

During his days as president, Thomas Jefferson and a group of companions were traveling across the country on horseback. They came to a river which had left its banks because of a recent downpour. The swollen river had washed the bridge away. Each rider was forced to ford the river on horseback, fighting for his life against the rapid currents. The very real possibility of death threatened each rider, which caused a traveler who was not part of their group to step aside and watch. After several had plunged in and made it to the other side, the stranger asked President Jefferson if he would ferry him across the river. The president agreed without hesitation. The man climbed on, and shortly thereafter the two of them made it safely to the other side. As the stranger slid off the back of the saddle onto dry ground, one in the group asked him, "Tell me, why did you select the president to ask this favor of?" The man was shocked, admitting he had no idea it was the president who had helped him. "All I know," he said, "is that on some of your faces was written the answer 'No,' and on some of them was the answer 'yes.' His was a 'Yes' face."

Freedom gives people a "Yes" face. I am confident Jesus had a "Yes" face. I have never seen Him, but I've determined from what I've read about Him that this was true. What a contrast He must have been! He was surrounded by lettered men, religious, robed, *righteous*, law-quoting, professional men whose very demeanor announced "NO!" Pious without, killers within . . . yet none of their poison seeped into His life. On the contrary, He revolutionized the entire direction of religion because He announced "Yes" while all His professional peers were frowning "No." That has intrigued me for years. How could it be? What was it that kept Him from getting caught in their grip? In one word, it was grace. He was so full of truth and grace, He left no inner space for their legalistic poison.

 REFLECTING ON GRACE

What do you think would be the most obvious characteristics of a "Yes" face?

Do you know someone who has a "Yes" face? How does being around that person make you feel?

The author pictures Jesus with a "Yes" face. Do you? Explain.

 AWAKENING TO GRACE

2 Corinthians 1:18–22

But as God is faithful, our word to you is not yes and no. For the Son of God, Christ Jesus, who was preached among you by us—by me and Silvanus and Timothy—was not yes and no, but is yes in Him. For as many as may be the promises of God, in Him they are yes; wherefore also through Him is our Amen to the glory of God through us. Now He who establishes us with you in Christ and anointed us is God, who also sealed us and gave us the Spirit in our hearts as a pledge.

In this passage, to what specific areas does "yes" apply?

Consider what each of the following results of God's "yes" means to you:

- You are established in Christ.

- You are anointed.

- You are sealed.

- You have been given the Spirit in your heart as a pledge.

WALKING IN GRACE

Considering the four areas listed above, in which ones do you need to accept God's "yes" toward you?

Do you think you have a "Yes" face? Why or why not?

How can you begin to develop a "Yes" face?

And the Word became flesh, and dwelt among us, and we saw His glory, glory as of the only begotten from the Father, full of grace and truth.

John 1:14

UNDERSTANDING GRACE

What exactly is grace? And is it limited to Jesus' life and ministry? You may be surprised to know that Jesus never used the word itself. He just taught it and, equally important, He lived it. Furthermore, the Bible never gives us a one-statement definition, though grace appears throughout its pages . . . not only the word itself but numerous demonstrations of it. Understanding what grace means requires our going back to an old Hebrew term that meant "to bend, to stoop." By and by, it came to include the idea of "condescending favor."

If you have traveled to London, you have perhaps seen royalty. If so, you may have noticed sophistication, aloofness, distance. On occasion, royalty in England will make the news because someone in the ranks of nobility will stop, kneel down, and touch or bless a commoner. That is grace.

There is nothing in the commoner that deserves being noticed or touched or blessed by the royal family. But because of grace in the heart of the queen, there is the desire at that moment to pause, to stoop, to touch, even to bless.

The late pastor and Bible scholar Donald Barnhouse perhaps said it best: "Love that goes upward is worship; love that goes outward is affection; love that stoops is grace."

To show grace is to extend favor or kindness to one who doesn't deserve it and can never earn it. Receiving God's acceptance by grace always stands in sharp contrast to earning it on the basis of works. Every time the thought of grace appears, there is the idea of its being undeserved. In no way is the recipient getting what he or she deserves. Favor is being extended simply out of the goodness of the heart of the giver.

REFLECTING ON GRACE

Describe an instance in your life when you received someone's unexpected act of grace.

Describe a time when you demonstrated God's grace by "bending down" for someone else.

As a way of understanding what Donald Barnhouse said (in the previous excerpt), narrow the scope of love to marital love, parental love, or Christian love. Then paraphrase his statement.

 AWAKENING TO GRACE

John 1:14–17

And the Word became flesh, and dwelt among us, and we beheld His glory, glory as of the only begotten from the Father, full of grace and truth. John testified about Him and cried out, saying, "This was He of whom I said, 'He who comes after me has a higher rank than I, for He existed before me.'" For of His fullness we have all received, and grace upon grace. For the Law was given through Moses; grace and truth were realized through Jesus Christ.

"Love that goes upward is worship; love that goes outward is affection; love that stoops is grace." How did Jesus illustrate the kind of love that John called "grace" in this passage?

How would you describe the difference between law and grace?

Write a brief explanation for each of these phrases:

"We have all received . . . grace upon grace."

"Grace and truth were realized through Jesus Christ."

WALKING IN GRACE

When you recognize God's grace toward you—His unearned favor—how do you feel?

Identify at least one conflict or difficult relationship that you believe would benefit from a gracious gesture on your part.

Pray for someone you know who struggles to accept or understand God's grace. What other ways can you help that person to encounter grace?

> *For the LORD God is a sun and shield; The LORD gives grace and glory; No good thing does He withhold from those who walk uprightly.*
>
> Psalm 84:11

GRACE: A MANY SPLENDORED THING

We use grace to describe many things in life:

- A well-coordinated athlete or dancer
- Good manners and being considerate of others
- Beautiful, well-chosen words
- Consideration and care for other people
- Various expressions of kindness and mercy

Those statements remind me of Christ. What a perfect illustration of grace! Think of several examples with me. He stood alongside a woman caught in adultery. The Law clearly stated, "Stone her." The grace killers who set her up demanded the same. Yet He said to those self-righteous Pharisees, "He who is without sin, let him cast the first stone." What grace! Under the Law they had every legal right to bury her beneath the rocks in their hands . . . and they were ready. There they stood with self-righteous fire in their eyes, but He intervened in grace.

When His friend Lazarus died, Martha met Him on the road and Mary later faced Him in the house. Both blamed Him for not coming earlier: "If You had been here, my brother would not have died!" There is strong accusation in those words. He took them in grace. With the turn of His hand, He could have sent them to eternity; but He refused to answer them back in argument. That is grace.

When He told stories, grace was a favorite theme. He employed a gracious style in handling children. He spoke of the prodigal son in grace. As He told stories of people who were caught in helpless situations, grace abounded . . . as with the good Samaritan. And instead of extolling the religious official who spoke of how proud God must be to have him in His family, Christ smiled with favor on the unnamed sinner who said, "God, be merciful to me, a sinner." Even from the cross He refused to be angry toward His enemies. Remember His prayer? "Father, forgive them . . ." No resentment, no bitterness. Amazing, this grace! Remarkable, the freedom and release it brought. And it came in full force from the only One on earth who had unlimited power, the Son of God.

 REFLECTING ON GRACE

Which of the descriptions of grace in the list on page 16 comes closest to your own understanding of the term? Why?

Choose one of the biblical examples given and explain how you see Jesus exercise grace in that instance.

What recurring failure or struggle in your life reminds you most painfully of your need for God's grace?

 AWAKENING TO GRACE

Luke 7:41–48 NLT

Then Jesus told him this story: "A man loaned money to two people—five hundred pieces of silver to one and fifty pieces to the other. But neither of them could repay him, so he kindly forgave them both, canceling their debts. Who do you suppose loved him more after that?"

Simon answered, "I suppose the one for whom he canceled the larger debt."

"That's right," Jesus said. Then he turned to the woman and said to Simon, "Look at this woman kneeling here. When I entered your home, you didn't offer me water to wash the dust from my feet, but she has washed them with her tears and wiped them with her hair. You didn't give me a kiss of greeting, but she has kissed my feet again and again from the time I first came in. You neglected the courtesy of olive oil to anoint my head, but she has anointed my feet with rare perfume. I tell you, her sins—and they are many—have been forgiven, so she has shown me much love. But a person who is forgiven little shows only little love." Then Jesus said to the woman, "Your sins are forgiven."

Although Jesus never used the word *grace*, it permeated His actions and words. How does this story of the woman illustrate the way grace affects people?

What were the three comparisons Jesus made between the way Simon treated Him and the way the woman treated Him?

Jesus left a fourth comparison incomplete, allowing Simon to fill in the gap. What was Jesus' final point?

WALKING IN GRACE

Grace is not grace unless it costs something. In Jesus' parable, it cost the money lender 550 pieces of silver. Describe a time when expressing grace turned out to be a costly gesture for you. Would you do it again?

Which of your attitudes or actions might be hindering your capacity to recognize grace in your relationship with God?

Make this last answer a subject of prayer today.

Surely He scorns the scornful, but gives grace to the humble.

Proverbs 3:34 NKJV

GRACE UNLIMITED

*M*y plea is that we not limit grace to Christ. We, too, can learn to be just as gracious as He. And since we can, we must, not only in our words and in great acts of compassion and understanding but in small ways as well. Let me describe four practical expectations you can anticipate as you get a firm grasp on grace.

First, *you can expect to gain a greater appreciation for God's gifts to you and others.* What gifts? Several come to mind. The free gift of salvation. The gift of life. The gift of laughter, of music, of beauty, of friendship, of forgiveness. Those who claim the freedom God offers gain an appreciation for the gifts that come with life.

Second, *you can expect to spend less time and energy critical of and concerned about others' choices.* Wouldn't that be a refreshing relief? When you get a grasp on grace—when you begin to operate in a context of freedom—you become increasingly less petty. You will allow

21

others room to make their own decisions in life, even though you may choose otherwise.

Third, *you can expect to become more tolerant and less judgmental.* Externals will not mean as much to you. You'll begin to cultivate a desire for authentic faith rather than endure a religion based on superficial performance. You will find yourself so involved in your own pursuit of grace, you'll no longer lay guilt trips on those with whom you disagree.

Fourth, *you can expect to take a giant step toward maturity.* As your world expands, thanks to an awakening of your understanding of grace, your maturity will enlarge. Before your very eyes, new vistas will open. It will be so transforming, you will never be the same.

REFLECTING ON GRACE

Which of the four results to the practice of grace listed above do you most long to see in the way you relate to others?

Why do you think it is so important to speak about the action of grace as "gifts"?

How does a deeper understanding of grace help people grow more spiritually mature?

AWAKENING TO GRACE

Colossians 1:3–6 NKJV

We give thanks to the God and Father of our Lord Jesus Christ, praying always for you, since we heard of your faith in Christ Jesus and of your love for all the saints; because of the hope which is laid up for you in heaven, of which you heard before in the word of the truth of the gospel, which has come to you, as it has also in all the world, and is bringing forth fruit, as it is also among you since the day you heard and knew the grace of God in truth.

How does Paul explain the results of grace to the believers in Colosse?

To what does this passage point as the source for hearing and understanding grace?

Looking at the way Paul begins his letter to fellow believers, what does this passage reveal to you about his gracious attitude?

WALKING IN GRACE

Rewrite into your own words each of the four results of exercising grace from today's reading.

1.

2.

3.

4.

Would a person spending time with you yesterday have known you live under God's grace? Why or why not?

In what ways can you aim for more grace-worthy attitudes today?

Write a note to a Christian friend expressing your gratitude for his or her faith and your joy in knowing that he or she understands God's grace.

DAY 6

It is God who saved us and chose us to live a holy life. He did this not because we deserved it, but because that was his plan long before the world began—to show his love and kindness to us through Christ Jesus.

2 Timothy 1:9 NLT

BONUS

Most people I know look forward to payday. You do too, right? For a week, or perhaps a two-week period, you give time and effort to your job. When payday arrives, you receive a hard-earned, well-deserved paycheck. I have never met anyone who bows and scrapes before his boss, saying, "Thank you. Oh, thank you for this wonderful, undeserved gift. How can I possibly thank you enough for my paycheck?" If we did, he would probably faint. Certainly, he would think, *What is wrong with this guy?* Why? Because your paycheck is not a gift. You've earned it. You deserve it. Cash it! Spend it! Save it! Invest it! Give it! After all, you had it coming. In the workplace, where wages are negotiated and agreed upon, there is no such thing as grace. We earn what we receive; we work for it. The wage "is not reckoned as a favor but as what is due."

But with God the economy is altogether different. There is no wage relationship with God. Spiritually speaking, you and I haven't earned anything but death. Like it or not, we are absolutely bankrupt, without eternal hope, without spiritual merit; we have nothing in ourselves that gives us favor in the eyes of our holy and righteous heavenly Father. So there's nothing we can earn that would cause Him to raise His eyebrows and say, "Now maybe you deserve eternal life with Me." No way. In fact, the individual whose track record is morally pure has no better chance at earning God's favor than the individual who has made a wreck and waste of his life and is currently living in unrestrained disobedience. Everyone who hopes to be eternally justified must come to God the same way: on the basis of grace; it is a gift. And that gift comes to us absolutely free. Any other view of salvation is heresy, plain and simple.

 REFLECTING ON GRACE

Looking back on your own track record, in what ways have you tried to *earn* God's grace?

What does it mean to you that grace cannot be earned—
that your salvation is a *free gift*?

What type of behavior by other people might make you
raise your eyebrows and discount them from God's grace?

 Awakening to Grace

Matthew 20:1–16

*For the kingdom of heaven is like a landowner
who went out early in the morning to hire laborers for his vineyard. When he had agreed with
the laborers for a denarius for the day, he sent
them into his vineyard. And he went out about
the third hour and saw others standing idle in
the market place; and to those he said, "You
also go into the vineyard, and whatever is right
I will give you." And so they went. Again he
went out about the sixth and the ninth hour,
and did the same thing. And about the eleventh
hour he went out, and found others standing
around; and he said to them, "Why have you
been standing here idle all day long?" They*

said to him, "Because no one hired us." He said to them, "You go into the vineyard too."

When evening came, the owner of the vineyard said to his foreman, "Call the laborers and pay them their wages, beginning with the last group to the first." When those hired about the eleventh hour came, each one received a denarius. When those hired first came, they thought that they would receive more; but each of them also received a denarius. When they received it, they grumbled at the landowner, saying, "These last men have worked only one hour, and you have made them equal to us who have borne the burden and the scorching heat of the day." But he answered and said to one of them, "Friend, I am doing you no wrong; did you not agree with me for a denarius? Take what is yours and go your way, but I wish to give to this last man the same as to you. Is it not lawful for me to do what I wish with what is my own? Or is your eye envious because I am generous?" So thus the last shall be first, and the first last.

Fairness is still an important issue today. How much of your spiritual life is focused on whether God has been fair to you?

In this passage, what is the relationship between grace and fairness? Do you think they are opposing concepts?

With which group of workers in this passage do you most identify? Why?

ᘏ WALKING IN GRACE

Think of a time when you saw a friend bestow grace upon someone. How did you react? If you felt bitterness, how could you have reacted differently?

For which of your actions do you expect to receive a reward from God?

In what specific ways has God been gracious to you today?

DAY 7

Can we boast, then, that we have done anything to be accepted by God? No, because our acquittal is not based on our good deeds. It is based on our faith.

Romans 3:27 NLT

GRACE FOR THE SINFUL

*F*or the next few moments, graze slowly over this paragraph of truth recorded by Paul in the letter to the Ephesians. Take your time. Don't hurry.

And you were dead in your trespasses and sins, in which you formerly walked according to the course of this world, according to the prince of the power of the air, of the spirit that is now working in the sons of disobedience. Among them we too all formerly lived in the lusts of our flesh, indulging the desires of the flesh and of the mind, and were by nature children of wrath, even as the rest. But God, being rich in mercy, because of His great love with which He loved us, even when we were dead in our transgressions, made

> us alive together with Christ (by grace you have
> been saved), and raised us up with Him, and seat-
> ed us with Him in the heavenly places, in Christ
> Jesus, in order that in the ages to come He might
> show the surpassing riches of His grace in kind-
> ness toward us in Christ Jesus. For by grace you
> have been saved through faith; and that not of
> yourselves, it is the gift of God; not as a result of
> works, that no one may boast. (Ephesians 2:1–9)

Pay close attention to ten single-syllable words, "by grace through faith . . . it is the gift of God."

One of my greatest anticipations is some glorious day being in a place where there will be no boasting, no name-dropping, no selfishness. Guess where it will be? Heaven. There will be no spiritual-sounding testimonies that call attention to somebody's super-colossal achievements. None of that! Everybody will have written across his or her life the word "Grace."

"How did you get up here?"

"Grace!"

"What made it possible?"

"Grace."

"What's your name?"

"Grace."

⬥ REFLECTING ON GRACE

When you share your spiritual autobiography with others, how much of it is based on what you've done and how much on what God's done?

In what ways has God's grace given you courage to honestly tell others about your life experiences?

Think of several common "spiritual-sounding" phrases (for example: "God changed my life" or "I'm blessed"). Choose two or three of your favorite phrases and ask yourself, "What would I say if someone asked me what I mean when I say this?"

⬥ AWAKENING TO GRACE

Jeremiah 9:23–26

Thus says the LORD, "Let not a wise man boast of his wisdom, and let not the mighty man boast of his might, let not a rich man boast of his riches; but let him who boasts boast of this, that he understands and knows Me, that I am

> the LORD who exercises lovingkindness, justice
> and righteousness on earth; for I delight in
> these things," declares the LORD.
>
> "Behold, the days are coming," declares the
> LORD, "that I will punish all who are circum-
> cised and yet uncircumcised—Egypt and
> Judah, and Edom and the sons of Ammon, and
> Moab and all those inhabiting the desert who
> clip the hair on their temples; for all the nations
> are uncircumcised, and all the house of Israel
> are uncircumcised of heart."

According to the passage, what are the three most likely topics people boast about? Which one do you struggle with the most?

Even the people of Judah, who were called God's people, still were "uncircumcised of heart." How does the second paragraph above indicate that external symbols and rituals are not the same as knowing God?

If these verses were written today, what modern religious rituals or identifying symbols might be mentioned as merely external forms of "circumcision"?

 WALKING IN GRACE

Describe an event in your life that taught you a memorable lesson about God's character. What did you learn?

What do you regard as your greatest accomplishment in life? How would you react if someone else received all the recognition for that achievement?

What happens to God's grace when you begin to show off or take credit for changes that God's grace has produced in you? In what ways could you boast about His grace in the presence of others?

You may say, "I am allowed to do anything." But I reply, "Not everything is good for you." And even though "I am allowed to do anything," I must not become a slave to anything.

1 Corinthians 6:12 NLT

THE RISK IN GRACE

*I*s grace risky? You bet your life it is. I am well aware that this issue of grace is indeed controversial; especially when I am calling for a new awakening to the freedom Christians have in Christ. A few will take what I write about grace and go crazy with it. Others will misread what I write, and misquote me, misunderstand me, and charge me with caring little about the holiness of God because (they will say) I give people the freedom to sin. On the other hand, some in the camp of carnality will thank me for relieving their guilt, because in their misunderstanding they now think it is okay for them to continue in their loose and carefree lifestyle. I wish these things would not occur, but that is the chance I'm willing to take by holding nothing back in order that the full message of grace be set forth. Yes, grace that is presented in all its charm and beauty is risky. It brings grace abusers as well as grace killers out from under the rocks!

Let's return to a key verse of Scripture, Romans 5:1: "Therefore, having been justified by faith, we have peace with God through our Lord Jesus Christ."

In order for anyone to stand securely and be at peace before a holy and just God, that person must be righteous. Hence, our need for justification. Remember the definition of justification? It is the sovereign act of God whereby He declares righteous the believing sinner while still in his sinning state. It doesn't mean that the believing sinner stops sinning. It doesn't even mean that the believing sinner is *made* righteous in the sense of suddenly becoming perpetually perfect. The sinner is *declared* righteous. God sovereignly bestows the gift of eternal life on the sinner at the moment he believes and thereby declares him righteous while the sinner still lives a life marked by periodic sinfulness. He hasn't joined a church. He hasn't started paying tithes. He hasn't given up all to follow Christ. He hasn't been baptized. He hasn't promised to live a sacrificial, spotlessly pure life. He has simply taken the gift of eternal life. He has changed his mind toward Christ (repentance) and accepted the free gift of God apart from works. Period. Transaction completed. By grace, through faith alone, God declares the sinner righteous (justification), and from that moment on the justified sinner begins a process of growth toward maturity (sanctification). Day by day, bit by bit, he learns what it means to live a life that honors Christ. But immediately? No way.

Please understand, to be justified does not mean "just as if I'd never sinned." I hear that often and it always troubles me. In fact, it weakens the full impact of justification. Justification really means this: Even though I still sin periodically and have found myself unable to stop sinning on a permanent basis—God declared me righteous when I believed. And because I will continue to sin from time to time, I find all the more reason to be grateful for grace. As a sinner I deserve vengeance. As a sinner I'm afraid of justice. And so, as a sinner, my only hope for survival is grace. In its purest form, it makes no earthly sense!

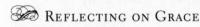 REFLECTING ON GRACE

Why is grace risky?

Describe how grace killers and grace abusers react to the concept of grace. Do you know anyone like this?

How would you explain the concepts of justification and sanctification to a new believer?

 AWAKENING TO GRACE

Romans 6:15–18

What then? Shall we sin because we are not under law but under grace? May it never be! Do you not know that when you present yourselves to someone as slaves for obedience, you are slaves of the one whom you obey, either of sin resulting in death, or of obedience resulting in righteousness? But thanks be to God that though you were slaves of sin, you became obedient from the heart to that form of teaching to which you were committed, and having been freed from sin, you became slaves of righteousness.

Which kind of grace abuser is Paul cautioning against in this passage?

Explain what it means to be a slave of righteousness.

Describe your vision of total freedom. How does your picture mesh with this passage?

WALKING IN GRACE

What prerequisites do you expect of others before you acknowledge or believe they have been saved? After what you've read so far, do you need to change your thinking? Why or why not?

When it comes to God's grace, how can you reach a balance between killing it and abusing it?

Think of your own process of spiritual growth toward maturity. What are two major lessons God has taught you on your path to sanctification?

1.

2.

I have swept away your sins like the morning mists. I have scattered your offenses like the clouds. Oh, return to me, for I have paid the price to set you free.

Isaiah 44:22 NLT

ALTERNATIVES TO GRACE

*I*f I choose not to risk, if I go the "safe" route and determine not to promote either salvation by grace or a lifestyle of grace, what are the alternatives? Four come to my mind, all of which are popular these days.

1.   *I can emphasize works over grace.* I can tell you that as a sinner you need to have a stronger commitment to Christ, demonstrated by the work you do in His behalf, before you can say that you truly believe. My problem in doing so is this: A sinner cannot commit to anything. He or she is spiritually dead, *remember?* There is no capacity for commitment in an unregenerate heart. Becoming an obedient, submissive disciple of Christ follows believing in Christ. Works *follow* faith. Behavior *follows* belief. Fruit comes *after* the tree is well rooted. Martin Luther's words come to mind:

No one can be good and do good unless God's grace first makes him good; and no one becomes good by works, but good works are done only by him who is good. Just so the fruits do not make the tree, but the tree bears the fruit. . . . Therefore all works, no matter how good they are and how pretty they look, are in vain if they do not flow from grace.

2.   *I can opt for giving you a list of dos and don'ts.* The list comes from my personal and/or traditional preferences. It becomes my responsibility to tell you what to do or not to do and why. I then set up the conditions by which you begin to earn God's acceptance through me. You do what I tell you to do . . . you don't do what I tell you not to do, and you're "in." You fail to keep the list, you're "out." This legalistic style of strong-arm teaching is one of the most prevalent methods employed in evangelical circles. Grace is strangled in such a context. To make matters worse, those in authority are so intimidating, their authority is unquestioned. Rare are those with sufficient strength to confront the list-makers.

3.   *I can leave no room for any gray areas.* Everything is either black or white, right or wrong. And as a result, the leader maintains strict control over the followers. Fellowship is based on whether there is full agreement. Herein lies the tragedy. This self-righteous, rigid standard becomes more

important than relationships with individuals. We first check out where people stand on the issues, and then we determine whether we will spend much time with them. The bottom line is this: We want to be *right* (as we see it, of course) more than we want to love our neighbors as ourselves. At that point our personal preferences eclipse any evidence of love. I am of the firm conviction that where grace exists, so must various areas of gray.

4. *I can cultivate a judgmental attitude toward those who may not agree or cooperate with my plan.* Grace killers are notorious for a judgmental attitude. It is perhaps the single most un-Christlike characteristic in evangelical circles today.

A quick glance back through the time tunnel will prove beneficial. Jesus found Himself standing before the brain trust of legalism, the Pharisees. Listening to Him were also many who believed in Him. He had been presenting His message to the crowd; it was a message of hope, of forgiveness, of freedom.

"As He spoke these things, many came to believe in Him. So Jesus was saying to those Jews who had believed Him, 'If you continue in My word, then you are truly disciples of Mine; and you will know the truth, and the truth will make you free'" (John 8:30–32).

He spoke of the liberating power of the truth. Even though the official grace killers rejected His message, He assured them it could make them free. All who embrace grace become "free indeed."

Free from what? Free from oneself. Free from guilt and shame. Free from the damnable impulses I couldn't stop when I was in bondage to sin. Free from the tyranny of others' opinions, expectations, demands. And free to what? Free to obey. Free to love. Free to forgive others as well as myself. Free to allow others to be who they are—different from me! Free to live beyond the limitations of human effort. Free to serve and glorify Christ. In no uncertain terms, Jesus Christ assured His own that His truth was able to liberate them from every needless restriction: "So if the Son makes you free, you will be free indeed" (John 8:36). I love that. The possibilities are unlimited.

⊗ REFLECTING ON GRACE

Which of the four alternatives to grace described above have you experienced in the past? What spirit was cultivated by such approaches?

What is the danger inherent in each of these alternatives?

Picture yourself completely unhampered by these four alternatives to grace. What would this freedom feel like to you? How would it transform your daily life?

 AWAKENING TO GRACE

Galatians 5:1–9

It was for freedom that Christ set us free; therefore keep standing firm and do not be subject again to a yoke of slavery.

Behold I, Paul, say to you that if you receive circumcision, Christ will be of no benefit to you. And I testify again to every man who receives circumcision, that he is under obligation to keep the whole Law. You have been severed from Christ, you who are seeking to be justified by law; you have fallen from grace. For we through the Spirit, by faith, are waiting for the hope of righteousness. For in Christ Jesus neither circumcision nor uncircumcision means anything, but faith working through love.

You were running well; who hindered you

from obeying the truth? This persuasion did not
come from Him who calls you. A little leaven
leavens the whole lump of dough.

What alternative to grace was being pushed on the
Galatians by certain grace killers?

According to Paul's warning, what would happen to God's
grace if the people followed the grace killers' advice?

Consider the actions and appearance you expect of other
Christians. How do your requirements interfere with
God's grace?

WALKING IN GRACE

List the aspects of freedom Swindoll mentioned in the last paragraph of the chapter text.
I am free from:

I am free to:

Which aspect of freedom you listed resonates with you the most? Why?

As someone who is "free to live beyond the limitations of human effort," how will you allow your life to demonstrate that grace today?

*It's like this: When I was a child, I
spoke and thought and reasoned as a
child does. But when I grew up, I put
away childish things.*

1 Corinthians 13:11 NLT

THE INESCAPABLE TENSION

*B*ecause of grace we have been freed from sin, from
its slavery, its bondage in our attitude, in our urges,
and in our actions. But having been freed and now living
by grace, we can actually go too far, set aside all self-
control, and take our liberty to such an extreme that we
again serve sin. But that isn't liberty at all, that's license.
And knowing of that possibility, many opt for legalism lest
they be tempted to live irresponsibly. Bad choice. How
much better to have such an awesome respect for the Lord
we voluntarily hold back as we apply self-control.

I remember when I first earned my license to drive. I
was about sixteen, as I recall. I'd been driving off and on
for three years (scary thought, isn't it?). My father had
been with me most of the time during my learning experiences, calmly sitting alongside me in the front seat, giving
me tips, helping me know what to do. My mother usually

wasn't in on those excursions because she spent more of her time biting her nails (and screaming) than she did advising. My father was a little more easygoing. Loud noises and screeching brakes didn't bother him nearly as much. My grandfather was the best of all. When I would drive his car, I would hit things . . . *Boom!* He'd say stuff like, "Just keep on going, Bud. I can buy more fenders, but I can't buy more grandsons. You're learning." What a great old gentleman. After three years, I finally earned my license.

I'll never forget the day I came in, flashed my newly acquired permit, and said, "Dad, look!" He goes, "Whoa! Look at this. You got your license. Good for you!" Holding the keys to his car, he tossed them in my direction and smiled, "Tell you what, son . . . you can have the car for two hours, all on your own." Only four words, but how wonderful: "All on your own."

I thanked him, danced out to the garage, opened the car door, and shoved the key into the ignition. My pulse rate must have shot up to 180 as I backed out of the driveway and roared off. While cruising along "all on my own," I began to think wild stuff—like, *This car can probably do 100 miles an hour. I could go to Galveston and back twice in two hours if I averaged 100 miles an hour. I can fly down the Gulf Freeway and even run a few lights. After all, nobody's here to say*, "*Don't!*" We're talking dangerous, crazy thoughts! But you know what? I didn't do any of them. I don't believe I drove above the speed limit. In fact, I distinctly remember turning into the driveway early . . . didn't even stay away the full two hours. Amazing, huh? I had my dad's car all to myself with a full gas tank in a context of total privacy and freedom, but I didn't go crazy. Why? My relationship with my dad and my granddad was so strong that I couldn't, even though I had a license and nobody was in the car to restrain me. Over a period of time there had developed a sense of trust, a deep love relationship that held me in restraint.

After tossing me the keys, my dad didn't rush out and tape a sign on the dashboard of the car, "Don't you dare drive beyond the speed limit" or "Cops are all around the city, and they'll catch you, boy, so don't even think about taking a risk." He simply smiled and said, "Here are the keys, son, enjoy it." What a demonstration of grace. And did *I* ever enjoy *it!* Looking back, now that I'm a father who has relived the same scene on four different occasions with my own children, I realize what a risk my father had taken.

REFLECTING ON GRACE

How do you distinguish between liberty, license, and legalism?

Why do you think many believers opt for legalism? Why does the author say this is a bad choice?

Think of a time that someone's demonstration of grace and love "held you in restraint."

 AWAKENING TO GRACE

1 Corinthians 3:1–4 NLT

Dear brothers and sisters, when I was with you I couldn't talk to you as I would to mature Christians. I had to talk as though you belonged to this world or as though you were infants in the Christian life. I had to feed you with milk and not with solid food, because you couldn't handle anything stronger. And you still aren't ready, for you are still controlled by your own sinful desires. You are jealous of one another and quarrel with each other. Doesn't that prove you are controlled

> *by your own desires? You are acting like people*
> *who don't belong to the Lord. When one of you*
> *says, "I am a follower of Paul," and another says,*
> *"I prefer Apollos," aren't you acting like those*
> *who are not Christians?*

In the above passage, what specific things were the Corinthians doing that told Paul they were being controlled by their sinful desires?

Replace the names "Paul" and "Apollos" with current Christian denominations (including your own). How often are you involved in these kinds of arguments?

Paul describes immature believers. How would he describe mature Christians?

✍ WALKING IN GRACE

What person has been most influential in shaping your beliefs? To what degree have you put that person's teachings through an honest evaluation?

How willing are you to question your most basic beliefs and let God's truth unfold?

Give yourself permission today to do something freeing—purely out of love for God, regardless of what other people think.

Describe something your past legalistic attitude prevented you from doing but which your new attitude of grace gives you the freedom to do.

*Blessed are those who do not con-
demn themselves by doing something
they know is all right.*

Romans 14:22 NLT

PRACTICAL SUGGESTIONS FOR GUARDING AGAINST EXTREMES

*T*hree suggestions come to mind as I think about living with the risks of grace and putting all this into balanced living.

First, *guard against extremes if you want to enjoy the freedom grace provides*. Try your best to keep balanced, then enjoy it. No reason to feel guilty. No reason to be afraid. Try this first: Simply give yourself permission to be free. Don't go crazy . . . but neither should you spend time looking over your shoulder worrying about those who "spy out your liberty," and wondering what they will think and say.

Second, *treat grace as an undeserved privilege rather than an exclusive right*. This will also help you keep a balance. Live gratefully, not arrogantly. Have fun, but don't flaunt. It is all in one's attitude, isn't it? It has nothing to do with financial status or where you live or what clothes you prefer or which car you drive. It has everything to do with attitude.

Third, *remember that while grace came to you freely, it cost the Savior His life*. It may seem free, but it was terribly expensive when He purchased it for us. And who wouldn't want to be free, since we have been purchased from the horrors of bondage?

Grace is God's universal good news of salvation. The tragedy is that some continue to live lives in a deathlike bog because they have been so turned off by a message that is full of restrictions, demands, negativism, and legalism. You may have been one of those held in bondage, victimized by a system that has stolen your joy and snuffed out your hope. If so, I have some wonderful news. You've gotten very close to the border. There's a flag flying. And on that flag is a cross. And if you come into this camp of grace beneath the cross, you'll never have to be in that awful bog again.

You will be free . . . *free at last*.

 REFLECTING ON GRACE

What are some habits or actions that help you lead a balanced life?

Take time to monitor your attitude this week. How often do you drift to extremes? When are you most balanced?

If you have been in "a deathlike bog" because of restrictions placed on you by legalism, what steps will you take to move out of the bog and into the "camp of grace beneath the cross"?

AWAKENING TO GRACE

Philippians 2:1–11

Therefore if there is any encouragement in Christ, if there is any consolation of love, if there is any fellowship of the Spirit, if any affection and compassion, make my joy complete by being of the same mind, maintaining the same love, united in spirit, intent on one purpose. Do nothing from selfishness or empty conceit, but with humility of mind regard one another as more important than yourselves; do not merely look out for your own personal interests, but also for the interests of others. Have this attitude in yourselves which was also in Christ Jesus, who, although He existed in the form of

*God, did not regard equality with God a thing
to be grasped, but emptied Himself, taking the
form of a bond-servant, and being made in the
likeness of men. Being found in appearance as
a man, He humbled Himself by becoming obedient to the point of death, even death on a
cross. For this reason also, God highly exalted
Him, and bestowed on Him the name which is
above every name, that at the name of Jesus
EVERY KNEE WILL BOW, of those who are in
heaven and on earth and under the earth, and
that every tongue will confess that Jesus Christ
is Lord, to the glory of God the Father.*

Considering how Christians have so many varied opinions, what do you think Paul meant when he told believers to be of "the same mind"? What is our "one purpose"?

What practical instructions are given to those who desire
to live a gracious life?

In this passage, what does Paul reveal about Christ's attitude? How did this attitude affect His actions?

᪥ WALKING IN GRACE

Into what kind of extremes are you most likely to fall? Are there certain steps you can take now to avoid turning away from God's grace?

Grace should be enjoyed! Describe how you last truly enjoyed this gift from God.

Identify at least one person who would benefit from hearing about the freedom of God's grace. How can you share His grace with that person today.

Day 12

But by the grace of God I am what I am, and His grace toward me did not prove vain.

1 Corinthians 15:10

Undeserving, yet Unconditionally Loved

Whatever he became, according to his own statement, Paul owed it all to "the grace of God." When I ponder the words from that grand apostle, I come up with what we might call his credo. We can reduce it to three single-syllable statements, the first consisting of only eight words; the second, ten words; and the third, twelve. Occasionally, it helps to take a profound, multifaceted theological truth and define it in simple, nontechnical terms.

First statement: *God does what He does by His grace.* Paul's first claim for being allowed to live, to say nothing of being used as a spokesman and leader, was "by the grace of God." Paul deserved the severest kind of judgment, but God gave the man His grace instead. Humanly speaking, Paul should have been made to endure incredible suffering for all the pain and heartache he had caused others. But he didn't, because God exhibited His grace.

That leads us to the second statement: *I am what I am by the grace of God.* It is as if he were admitting, "If there is any goodness now found in me, I deserve none of the glory; grace gets the credit."

In our day of high-powered self-achievement and an overemphasis on the importance of personal accomplishments and building one's own ego-centered kingdom, this idea of giving grace the credit is a much-needed message. How many people who reach the pinnacle of their career say to the *Wall Street Journal* reporter or in an interview in *Business Week,* "I am what I am by the grace of God"? How many athletes would say that kind of thing at a banquet in his or her honor? What a shocker it would be today if someone were to say, "Don't be impressed at all with me. My only claim to fame is the undeserved grace of God." Such candor is rare.

There's a third statement, which seems to be implied in Paul's closing statement: *I let you be what you are by the grace of God.* Grace is not something simply to be claimed; it is meant to be demonstrated. It is to be shared, used as a basis for friendships, and drawn upon for sustained relationships.

Jesus spoke of an abundant life that we enter into when we claim the freedom He provides by His grace. Wouldn't it be wonderful if people cooperated with His game plan?

There is nothing to be compared to grace when it comes to freeing others from bondage.

 REFLECTING ON GRACE

Describe one thing that God has done for you that reveals His awesome grace.

List four major accomplishments in your life. After each write Paul's statement, "I am what I am by the grace of God." In what ways does this exercise change your view of these successes?

1.

2.

3.

4.

What relationship in your life will be most profoundly affected if you decide to let that person be what he or she is by the grace of God?

AWAKENING TO GRACE

1 Corinthians 15:9–11

For I am the least of the apostles, and not fit to be called an apostle, because I persecuted the church of God. But by the grace of God I am what I am, and His grace toward me did not prove vain; but I labored even more than all of them, yet not I, but the grace of God with me. Whether then it was I or they, so we preach and so you believed.

Paul's history did not disappear when he became a Christian. How does Paul use his past failures to promote deeper understanding of the grace of God?

In the passage, what did Paul mean when he says, "His grace toward me did not prove vain"?

Do you ever feel unfit for the tasks God has given you? How can God's grace help you?

WALKING IN GRACE

Using the statement, "I am what I am by the grace of God," write your own personalized statement regarding how God's grace affects your life.

To what person do you need to apply the words of the third statement, "I let you be what you are by the grace of God"? Explain.

Most New Testament writers mention the grace of God in both the greeting and closing of their letters. Using this model in your letters and e-mails, practice greeting people with a simple blessing of grace.

Day 13

Who will free me from this life that is dominated by sin? Thank God! The answer is in Jesus Christ our Lord.

Romans 7:24–25 NLT

Defining Liberty

Without becoming needlessly academic, I want to define a term that I've been tossing around. What do I mean when I declare that the Christian has *liberty?* Essentially, liberty is freedom . . . freedom from something and freedom to do something.

Liberty is freedom from slavery or bondage. It is initially freedom from sin's power and guilt. Freedom from God's wrath. Freedom from satanic and demonic authority. And equally important, it is freedom from shame that could easily bind me, as well as freedom from the tyranny of others' opinions, obligations, and expectations.

There was a time in my life without Christ when I had no freedom from the urges and impulses within me. I was at the mercy of my master Satan and sin was my lifestyle. When the urges grew within me, I had nothing to hold me in check, nothing to restrain me. It was an awful bondage.

For example, in my personal life I was driven by jealousy for many miserable years. It was consuming. I served it not unlike a slave serves a master. Then there came a day when I was spiritually awakened to the charming grace of God and allowed it to take full control, and almost before I knew it the jealousy died. And I sensed for the first time, perhaps in my whole life, true love; the joy, the romance, the spontaneity, the free-flowing creativity brought about by the grace of a faithful wife, who would love me no matter what, who was committed to me in faithfulness for all her life. That love and that commitment motivated me to love in return more freely than ever. I no longer loved out of fear that I would lose her, but I loved out of the joy and the blessing connected with being loved unconditionally and without restraint.

Now that Christ has come into my life and I have been awakened to His grace, He has provided a freedom from that kind of slavery to sin. And along with that comes a freedom that brings a fearlessness, almost a sense of invincibility in the presence of the adversity. This power, keep in mind, is because of Christ, who lives within me.

In addition, He has also brought a glorious freedom from the curse of the Law. By that I mean freedom from the constancy of its demands to perform in order to please God and/or others. It is a freedom from the fear of condemnation before God as well as from an accusing conscience.

Freedom from the demands of other people, from all the *shoulds* and *oughts* of the general public.

Such freedom is *motivated*—motivated by unconditional love. When the grace of Christ is fully awake in your life, you find you're no longer doing something due to fear or out of shame or because of guilt, but you're doing it through love. The dreadful tyranny of performing in order to please someone is over . . . forever.

Grace also brings a freedom *to do* something else—a freedom to enjoy the rights and the privileges of being out from under slavery *and* allowing others such freedom. It's freedom to experience and enjoy a new kind of power that only Christ could bring. It is a freedom to become all that He meant me to be, *regardless of how He leads others*. I can be me—fully and freely. It is a freedom to know Him in an independent and personal way. And that freedom is then released to others so they can be who they are meant to be—different from me!

You see, God isn't stamping out little cookie-cutter Christians across the world so that we all think alike and look alike and sound alike and act alike. The body has variety. We were never meant to have the same temperaments and use the same vocabulary and wear the same syrupy smile and dress the same way and carry on the same ministry. I repeat: God is pleased with variety. This freedom to be who we are is nothing short of magnificent.

It is freedom to make choices, freedom to know His will, freedom to walk in it, freedom to obey His leading me in my life and you in your life. Once you've tasted such freedom, nothing else satisfies.

Perhaps I should reemphasize that it is a liberty you will have to fight for. Why? Because the ranks of Christianity are full of those who compare and would love to control and manipulate you so you will become as miserable as they are. After all, if they are determined to be "cramped, somber, dull, and listless," then they expect you to be that way, too. "Misery loves company" is the legalists' unspoken motto, though they never admit it.

REFLECTING ON GRACE

What are some of the most obvious differences between a person in legalistic bondage and a person who has freedom in Christ?

What difference does it make in your life to know that you are free from demands to perform—for God or for others?

God directs His liberty toward us and *through* us to others. How does God's liberty allow you to graciously offer freedom to other people?

AWAKENING TO GRACE

Therefore there is now no condemnation for those who are in Christ Jesus. For the law of the Spirit of life in Christ Jesus has set you free from the law of sin and of death. For what the Law could not do, weak as it was through the flesh, God did: sending His own Son in the likeness of sinful flesh and as an offering for sin, He condemned sin in the flesh, so that the requirement of the Law might be fulfilled in us, who do not walk according to the flesh, but according to the Spirit. For those who are according to the flesh set their minds on the things of the flesh, but those who are according to the Spirit, the things of the Spirit. For the mind set on the flesh is death, but the mind set on the Spirit is life and peace, because the mind set on the flesh is hostile toward God; for it does not subject itself to the law of God, for it is not even able to do so; and those who are in the flesh cannot please God.

However, you are not in the flesh but in the Spirit, if indeed the Spirit of God dwells in you. But if anyone does not have the Spirit of Christ, he does not belong to Him. If Christ is in you, though the body is dead because of sin, yet the spirit is alive because of righteousness. But if the Spirit of Him who raised Jesus from the dead dwells in you, He who raised Christ Jesus from the dead will also give life to your mortal bodies through His Spirit who dwells in you. So then, brethren, we are under obligation, not to the flesh, to live according to the flesh—for if you are living according to the flesh, you must die; but if by the Spirit you are putting to death the deeds of the body, you will live. For all who are being led by the Spirit of God, these are sons of God.

What does it mean that you face "no condemnation" and are "set free from the law of sin and death"?

Contrast Paul's descriptions of a life led by the Holy Spirit and one controlled by the sinful nature. What are the results of each?

How can you be sure that you are walking according to the Spirit?

ᴥ Walking in Grace

Consider how Christianity would fare across the globe if all Christians were "cookie-cutter Christians." How does diversity among believers help to reach many different types, ages, races, and backgrounds of people?

How does diversity in your own congregation help to spread the gospel message? (Or, how would more diversity help your church be more effective?)

What specifically will you do this week to allow others the freedom to be who God has called them to be?

For when I tried to keep the law, I realized I could never earn God's approval. So I died to the law so that I might live for God. I have been crucified with Christ.

Galatians 2:19 NLT

DEFINING LEGALISM

*I*n contrast to yesterday's thoughts on liberty, what does it mean to say that *legalism* puts people under bondage? Legalism is an attitude, a mentality based on pride. It is an obsessive conformity to an artificial standard for the purpose of exalting oneself. A legalist assumes the place of authority and pushes it to unwarranted extremes.

In so many words, legalism says, "I do this or I don't do that, and therefore I am pleasing God." Or, "If only I could do this or not do that, I would be pleasing to God." Or perhaps, "These things that I'm doing or not doing are the things I perform to win God's favor." They aren't spelled out in Scripture, you understand. They've been passed down or they have been dictated to the legalist and have become an obsession to him or her. Legalism is rigid, grim, exacting, and lawlike in nature. Pride, which is at the heart of legalism, works in sync with other motivating factors. Like guilt. And fear. And shame. It leads to an emphasis on what one should *not* be, and what one should *not* do. It flourishes in a drab context of negativism.

Let's get specific. The one place on earth where we would most expect to be set free is, in fact, the very place we are most likely to be placed into slavery: the church. What happened in the first century can surely happen in the twentieth. Paul writes the Galatians of his surprise: "You were running well; who hindered you from obeying the truth?"

Allow me to amplify his thought—"When I was with you, some of you were into the 100-meter dash, others were doing the 440 with ease. Still others were into much longer distances . . . you were marathoners. The truth freed you and I distinctly recall how well you were running as well as how much joy you demonstrated. Who cut in on your stride? Who took away your track shoes? Who told you that you shouldn't be running or enjoying the race? Some of you have stopped running altogether" (Swindoll paraphrase).

How many Christians do you know who exercise the joy and freedom to be a person full of life, living on tiptoe, enjoying spontaneous living—as opposed to the number-less hundreds of thousands who take their cues from the legalists and live life accordingly? Isn't it surprising to anyone who has been set free that anybody would ever want to return to bondage? Surely, that must grieve our God.

🐚 REFLECTING ON GRACE

Describe the daily life of a Christian. In your answer, however, you cannot use negative expressions ("A Christian doesn't . . ." or "A Christian shouldn't . . .") and you can't use positive expressions that describe only rituals ("A Christian goes to church" or "A Christian reads the Bible"). See if you can describe a life that captures the joyous freedom mentioned in the quotation above.

How do you think you personally please God? What does the Bible say is the only way to please God?

Why do you think some believers return to bondage after being set free in Christ?

✑ AWAKENING TO GRACE

Philippians 3:1–11

Finally, my brethren, rejoice in the Lord. To write the same things again is no trouble to me, and it is a safeguard for you.

Beware of the dogs, beware of the evil workers, beware of the false circumcision; for we are the true circumcision, who worship in the Spirit of God and glory in Christ Jesus and put no confidence in the flesh, although I myself might have confidence even in the flesh. If anyone else has a mind to put confidence in the flesh, I far more: circumcised the eighth day, of the nation of Israel, of the tribe of Benjamin, a Hebrew of Hebrews; as to the Law, a Pharisee; as to zeal, a persecutor of the church; as to the righteousness which is in the Law, found blameless.

But whatever things were gain to me, those things I have counted as loss for the sake of Christ. More than that, I count all things to be loss in view of the surpassing value of knowing Christ Jesus my Lord, for whom I have suffered the loss of all things, and count them but rubbish so that I may gain Christ, and may be found in Him, not having a righteousness of my

> *own derived from the Law, but that which is*
> *through faith in Christ, the righteousness*
> *which comes from God on the basis of faith,*
> *that I may know Him and the power of His res-*
> *urrection and the fellowship of His sufferings,*
> *being conformed to His death; in order that I*
> *may attain to the resurrection from the dead.*

How does Paul view his former "perfect" life compared with his life in Christ?

Paraphrase Paul's words to describe what might be your own "confidence in the flesh."

✌ WALKING IN GRACE

Considering the author's athletic metaphor, how well do you see yourself running the race? In what ways has legalism slowed your pace?

How much of your Christian walk is spent struggling through feelings of guilt, fear, and shame? What effect do these emotions have on your relationship with Jesus?

When you evaluate your life, to whom do you accredit your achievements, godliness, and success?

DAY 15

So Christ has really set us free. Now make sure that you stay free, and don't get tied up again in slavery to the law.

Galatians 5:1 NLT

FOUR ANTILEGALISTIC STRATEGIES

Grace killers cannot be mildly ignored or kindly tolerated. You can no more allow legalism to continue than you could permit a rattlesnake to slip into your house and hide. Before long, somebody is going to get hurt. So then, since liberty is worth fighting for, how do we do it? Where can our personal grace awakening begin? I can think of four strong strategies:

Keep standing firm in your freedom. I'm reminded of what Paul wrote in Galatians 5:1: "It was for freedom that Christ set us free; therefore keep standing firm and do not be subject again to a yoke of slavery." Stand your ground. Ask the Lord to give you courage.

Stop seeking the favor of everyone. This may be a stubborn habit to break, but it is really worth all the effort you can muster. If you're in a group where you feel you are being coerced to do certain things that are against your conscience or you're being pressured to stop doing things that you see no problem with, get out of the group! You're unwise to stay in situations where your conscience tells you it is not right. That is nothing more than serving men, not God. I don't care how spiritual sounding it may be, stop seeking the favor of everybody.

Start refusing to submit to bondage. Call it what it is: slavery. It's trying to be "spiritual" by performance. Think of how delightful it would be to get rid of all the anxiety that comes with the bondage to which you have submitted yourself; think how clean you could feel by being real again, or perhaps real for the first time in your adult life.

Continue being straightforward about the truth. That means live honestly. If you don't agree, say so kindly but firmly. If you are the only one, be true to yourself and stand alone. When you blow it, say, "I blew it." If you don't know, admit the truth. It's okay not to know. And the next time your kids spot hypocrisy, even though you may feel embarrassed, agree with them, "You know what, kids? You're right. I was a first-class hypocrite. What you saw and pointed out is exactly right." Tell them that. It may sound embarrassing to you now, but they will admire and respect your admission. And they won't grow up damaged. Best of all, they will learn to model the same kind of vulnerability and honesty, even if you are in vocational Christian work . . . *especially if you're in vocational Christian work.*

Nobody expects perfection, but they do and they should expect honesty.

We need affirmation and encouragement to be all we're meant to be, and because so many are rather delicate within, they need those who are strong to assist them in their fight for liberty. And so, if for no other reason, liberty is worth fighting for so others can breathe freely.

If fighting for liberty sounds too aggressive to you, perhaps too selfish, then think of it as fighting so others can be set free—so others can be awakened to the joys and privileges of personal freedom. Those who do that on real battlefields are called patriots or heroes. With all my heart, I believe those who square off against legalism should be considered the same.

✆ REFLECTING ON GRACE

Have you ever had to stand firm in your Christian freedom against legalists? Explain.

Of the four strategies mentioned above, which is the most difficult for you? Why?

In what areas of your life are you not living honestly?

 AWAKENING TO GRACE

Matthew 23:23–28

Woe to you, scribes and Pharisees, hypocrites! For you tithe mint and dill and cummin, and have neglected the weightier provisions of the law: justice and mercy and faithfulness; but these are the things you should have done without neglecting the others. You blind guides, who strain out a gnat and swallow a camel!

Woe to you, scribes and Pharisees, hypocrites! For you clean the outside of the cup and of the dish, but inside they are full of robbery and self-indulgence. You blind Pharisee, first clean the inside of the cup and of the dish, so that the outside of it may become clean also.

Woe to you, scribes and Pharisees, hypocrites! For you are like whitewashed tombs which on the outside appear beautiful, but inside they are full of dead men's bones and all uncleanness So you, too, outwardly appear righteous to men, but inwardly you are full of hypocrisy and lawlessness.

Jesus boldly compared the Pharisees with several objects to make a point. In your own words, write a brief explanation for each of Jesus' following metaphors.

The Pharisees as filthy cups:

The Pharisees as whitewashed tombs:

What guidelines did Jesus give the Pharisees to live more gracious lives?

❧ WALKING IN GRACE

Personally, what does it mean to you to live an honest life?

Whom do you know who has successfully stood firm in his or her freedom? Ask that person to support you in your battle against legalism.

Lift someone up in prayer this week who struggles with legalism and accepting God's grace. What are some simple ways you can exemplify God's freedom for that person?

So you should consider yourselves dead to sin and able to live for the glory of God through Christ Jesus.

Romans 6:11 NLT

CLAIMING OUR FREEDOM FROM SIN'S CONTROL

*I*n the wonderful sixth chapter of Romans, Paul presents three techniques for living by grace, above sin's domination. I find each one linked to a particular term he uses:

Know—"Or do you not know that all of us who have been baptized into Christ Jesus have been baptized into His death? . . . Knowing this, that our old self was crucified with Him, in order that our body of sin might be done away with, so that we should no longer be slaves to sin; . . . knowing that Christ, having been raised from the dead, is never to die again; death no longer is master over Him" (vv. 3, 6, 9).

Consider—"Even so consider yourselves to be dead to sin, but alive to God in Christ Jesus" (v. 11).

Present—"And do not go on presenting the members of your body to sin as instruments of unrighteousness; but present yourselves to God as those alive from the dead, and your members as instruments of righteousness to God" (v. 13).

In order for us to live free from sin's control, free from the old master, with the power to walk a new kind of life, we have to *know* something, we have to *consider* something, and we have to *present* something.

Christ died for us on the cross. He was raised from the dead for us at the tomb. When we believed in the Savior's death and resurrection, we were "dipped" into the same scene. Our identity was changed. We didn't feel it, we didn't see it, we didn't hear it, but it occurred, nevertheless. When we came to Christ, we were placed into Him as His death became ours, His victorious resurrection became ours, His "awakening" to new life became our "awakening," His powerful walk became our powerful walk. Before we can experience the benefits of all that, we have to *know* it. The Christian life is not stumbling along, hoping to keep up with the Savior. He lives in me and I live in Him. And in this identification with Him, His power becomes mine. His very life becomes my life, guaranteeing that His victory over sin is mine to claim. I no longer need to live as a slave to sin.

"Now if we have died with Christ, we believe that we shall also live with Him, knowing that Christ, having been raised from the dead, is never to die again; death no longer is master over Him. For the death that He died, He died to sin once for all; but the life that He lives, He lives to God" (vv. 8–10).

You will meet well-meaning Christians who teach about crucifying oneself. But I have good news for you: That has already been done. You are in Christ. He was crucified once for all. He died for you so you never need to die again. Because we have our identification with Him, we have all the power needed to live the rest of our lives above the drag and dregs of slavery. Death to sin is an accomplished act, a finished fact. Theoretically, it has all been taken care of. A victorious walk begins with our *knowing* this fact. Christ's "Emancipation Proclamation" has put to death the whole idea of slavery to sin. Having died to sin's power, we are now free to serve our new Master.

 REFLECTING ON GRACE

Explain briefly what you *know* about Jesus and what He has done for you.

Consider how it can be true that you are "dead to sin, but alive to God."

How can you *present* yourself to God as an "instrument of righteousness"?

 AWAKENING TO GRACE

Romans 11:33–12:2

Oh, the depth of the riches both of the wisdom and knowledge of God! How unsearchable are His judgments and unfathomable His ways! FOR WHO HAS KNOWN THE MIND OF THE LORD, OR WHO BECAME HIS COUNSELOR? Or WHO HAS FIRST GIVEN TO HIM THAT IT MIGHT BE PAID BACK TO HIM AGAIN? For from Him and through Him and to Him are all things. To Him be the glory forever. Amen.

Therefore I urge you, brethren, by the mercies of God, to present your bodies a living and holy sacrifice, acceptable to God, which is your spiritual service of worship. And do not be conformed to this world, but be transformed by the renewing of your mind, so that you may prove what the will of God is, that which is good and acceptable and perfect.

In what ways are you conformed to this world—either to the unredeemed world of sin or to the rule-filled world of legalists?

How does your mind need to be transformed?

What is the result of a transformed mind?

❧ WALKING IN GRACE

Christ's victory over sin is yours to claim! If you are waiting to claim it, for what are you waiting?

What does it mean for you personally to be "in Christ"?

How has your own life's journey reflected both the process of dying with Christ and living with Him?

And you will know the truth, and the truth will make you free.

John 8:32

GRACE AND FREEDOM

With all this talk about grace and liberty, perhaps it's time for me to clarify something. Some may be asking: Doesn't liberty have its limits? Shouldn't folks restrain their freedom and occasionally hold themselves in check? Yes, without question. Grace can be and sometimes is—abused. By that I mean exercising one's liberty without wisdom, having no concern over whether it offends or wounds a young and impressionable fellow believer. But I must hasten to add that I believe such restraint is an individual matter. It is not to be legislated, not something to be forced on someone else. Limitations are appropriate and necessary, but I fail to find in Scripture anyplace where one is to require such restraint from another. To do so is legalism. It plugs up breathing holes. It kills grace. The best restraint is self-restraint that comes from the inner prompting of the Holy Spirit through the person and presence of Jesus Christ in each individual life. It's been my observation over the last thirty years that the vast majority of believers need to be freed, not restrained. Our job is to free people; God's job is to restrain them. God is doing His job much better than we are doing ours.

I like to think of certain verses in Scripture as those that help us breathe. By that I mean they encourage true freedom. They liberate! I suggest that all who wish to be free—truly free from bondage traps and legalistic prisons—read these verses again and again and again. I would suggest you type them on three-by-five cards and tape them to your bathroom mirror. Read them aloud each morning. They will help awaken grace within you on a daily basis. Here are a few that I often quote and claim:

It was for freedom that Christ set us free. (Galatians 5:1)

For he who has died is freed from sin. (Romans 6:7)

For the law of the Spirit of life in Christ Jesus has set you free. (Romans 8:2)

What then shall we say to these things? If God is for us, who is against us? He who did not spare His own Son, but delivered Him over for us all, how will He not also with Him freely give us all things? (Romans 8:31–32)

So if the Son shall make you free, you will be free indeed. (John 8:36)

❧ REFLECTING ON GRACE

In what ways do you relate to the author's statement: "Our job is to free people; God's job is to restrain them"?

In the past, which of these jobs have you taken as your main responsibility? What were the results?

Which of the previous verses would be your first choice as a theme verse for your own desire to practice Christian freedom? Why?

❧ AWAKENING TO GRACE

Galatians 5:13–16

For you were called to freedom, brethren; only do not turn your freedom into an opportunity for the flesh, but through love serve one another. For the whole Law is fulfilled in one word, in the statement, "YOU SHALL LOVE YOUR NEIGHBOR

AS YOURSELF." *But if you bite and devour one
another, take care that you are not consumed by
one another.*

*But I say, walk by the Spirit, and you will
not carry out the desire of the flesh.*

How can freedom become an "opportunity for the flesh"?
What would keep that from happening?

Describe two or three "footsteps" that illustrate what it
means to "walk by the Spirit."

WALKING IN GRACE

How could you use your freedom in Christ today to serve
someone else in love?

What other ways can you think of for keeping those key
"freedom verses" in view besides typing them on cards and
taping them to a mirror?

What situations could you face today that will test your desire to walk by the Spirit as you live out your freedom in Christ?

DAY 18

*But fortunately God doesn't grade us
on our diet.*

1 Corinthians 8:8 MSG

FREE TO EAT, OR NOT

A funny thing happened to me recently. One of the sound-and-light people at the church where I pastor (a real character!) heard me teach on the subject of freedom. A couple of weeks later he pulled a gag on me. With an impish grin he said, "You had a birthday recently, didn't you?" I nodded yes. He said, "You're originally from Texas, right?" By now I knew I was in for something! "Yep," I answered. He said, "Well, I have something for you." He put a small can in my hand about the size of a can of snuff. It was a can of armadillo meat. I groaned. The label read, "Pure Texas Armadillo—sun-dried and road-tenderized." The ingredients were printed on the other side: "Pure sun-dried armadillo, run over by a log truck three miles south of Pollok, Texas. Not over 20 percent hair and gravel. May contain foreign matter."

He told me that since I was such a believer in grace, I was free to eat it. I thought, *Whoa! This will gag a maggot!* My point? Because of grace, my friend can eat armadillo

97

and I can eat armadillo. It's okay. It's fine if he wishes to, but it so happens that God has led me *not* to eat armadillo. (It's that "foreign matter" that concerns me.) But if you want to eat armadillo, that's great! Personally, I have my own personal list of dietary don'ts (which includes armadillo). You may not have that on your list, so in good Texas fashion, "git at it." I promise, I will not slander you or judge you as you munch on all that hair and gravel.

What in the world is all this about? Let me give it to you straight. Don't give me your personal list of dos and don'ts to live by! And you can count on this: I will never give you my personal list of dos and don'ts to follow! Being free means you have no reason whatsoever to agree with my personal list; nor should you slander me because it isn't exactly like yours. That is one of the ways Christians can live in harmony. It is called living by grace, and it is the only way to fly.

❧ REFLECTING ON GRACE

What eating habits or favorite foods set you a little apart in your family or among your friends?

How does good-natured kidding over eating habits feel different from unbending rules that are imposed by a group or person about any area of life?

How does it set you free not to have to live by someone else's dos and don'ts and not to have to expect them to live by yours?

 AWAKENING TO GRACE

1 Corinthians 8:8–13

But food will not commend us to God; we are neither the worse if we do not eat, nor the better if we do eat. But take care that this liberty of yours does not somehow become a stumbling block to the weak. For if someone sees you, who have knowledge, dining in an idol's temple, will not his conscience, if he is weak, be strengthened to eat things sacrificed to idols? For through your knowledge he who is weak is ruined, the brother for whose sake Christ died. And so, by sinning against the brethren and wounding their conscience when it is weak, you sin against Christ. Therefore, if food causes my

> *brother to stumble, I will never eat meat again,*
> *so that I will not cause my brother to stumble.*

Why doesn't food "commend us to God" (or as Eugene Peterson put it, "God doesn't grade us on our diet")?

In the context of this passage, how would eating meat have caused a fellow believer difficulty? What might be a modern parallel?

How is Paul exercising freedom by choosing not to eat something he has the right to eat?

WALKING IN GRACE

Almost any behavior or choice can be described as something that "might cause a brother or sister to stumble." How will you balance personal freedom in Christ with the importance of considering the weaknesses or needs of others?

What personal spiritual benefits have you experienced from giving up or limiting certain habits out of a desire to express consideration for others?

In what situations have you learned the personal value of having to preserve a right in spite of the "demands or weaknesses" of others?

DAY 19

You shall walk in all the way which the LORD your God has commanded you.

Deuteronomy 5:33

WHEN GOD SAYS DO OR DON'T

*N*ow you say, "Well, what if we find a list of dos and don'ts in Scripture?" That is a very different issue! Any specified list in Scripture is to be obeyed without hesitation or question. That's an inspired list for all of us to follow, not someone's personal list. Let me encourage you to guide your life by any and all Scripture with all of your heart, regardless of how anyone else may respond. But when questionable things aren't specified in Scripture, it then becomes a matter of one's personal preference or convictions.

God has given His children a wonderful freedom in Christ, which means not only freedom from sin and shame but also a freedom in lifestyle, so that we can become models of His grace. Being free, enjoying your liberty, and allowing others the same enjoyment is hard to do if you're insecure. It is especially hard to do if you were raised by legalistic parents and led by legalistic pastors with an oversensitive conscience toward pleasing everyone. Those kinds of parents and pastors can be ultracontrolling, manipulative, and judgmental. Frequently, they use the Bible as a hammer to pound folks into submission rather than as a guide to lead others into grace. Sometimes it takes years for people who have been under a legalistic cloud to finally have the courage to walk freely in the grace of God. Unfortunately, some who finally grasp this freedom go so far in it they abuse the grace of God by flaunting their liberty.

That can be just as tragic as those who don't go far enough. To return to one of my favorite words, we need the *balance*.

✍ Reflecting on Grace

Growing up, to what extent did legalism influence your walk with Christ? What was your response to this environment then and now?

Who can support you in maintaining balance as you emerge from a "legalistic cloud"?

Describe a time when others have used the Bible to guide you into grace. What happened? When have you used the Bible in this way?

Awakening to Grace

Romans 14:1–10

Now accept the one who is weak in faith, but not for the purpose of passing judgment on his opinions. One person has faith that he may eat all things, but he who is weak eats vegetables only. The one who eats is not to regard with contempt the one who does not eat, and the one who does not eat is not to judge the one who eats, for God has accepted him. Who are you to judge the servant of another? To his own master he stands or falls; and he will stand, for the Lord is able to make him stand.

One person regards one day above another, another regards every day alike. Each person must be fully convinced in his own mind. He who observes the day, observes it for the Lord, and he who eats, does so for the Lord, for he gives thanks to God; and he who eats not, for the Lord he does not eat, and gives thanks to God. For not one of us lives for himself, and not one dies for himself; for if we live, we live for the Lord, or if we die, we die for the Lord; therefore whether we live or die, we are the Lord's. For to this end Christ died and lived again, that He might be Lord both of the dead and of the living.

But you, why do you judge your brother? Or you again, why do you regard your brother with contempt? For we will all stand before the judgment seat of God.

According to Paul, what is the purpose of holding personal beliefs? How can you distinguish personal convictions from fundamental beliefs?

What is to be your attitude toward others regarding personal convictions?

In what ways does this attitude promote grace?

WALKING IN GRACE

Consider the last disagreement you had with another Christian. If it centered on a personal conviction, are there ways you could have responded more graciously?

How can you find "balance" in your Christian life?

If you were raised in a legalistic setting, what can you do to break this pattern so that it is not repeated with the next generation?

DAY 20

Choose to love the LORD your God and to obey him and commit yourself to him, for he is your life.

Deuteronomy 30:20 NLT

FREE TO CHOOSE FREEDOM

I wish I could guarantee all of us full freedom from sin 365 days a year, but that is not possible — not so long as we are earthbound. Perpetual sinlessness (theologians call it "sinless perfection") will not be ours to enjoy until we are given glorified bodies and we are at home in heaven. But the good news is that we don't have to sin on a constant, day-after-day basis. Grace has freed us to obey Christ.

But thanks be to God that though you were slaves of sin, you became obedient from the heart to that form of teaching to which you were committed, and having been freed from sin, you became slaves of righteousness. (Romans 6:17–18)

Wonderful, wonderful truth! Choosing righteousness, we enjoy a lifestyle marked by God's blessings, stability, and strength. Grace frees us to choose. We can decide to walk with God and draw strength from Him to face whatever life throws at us. Or we can decide to walk away from God and face the inescapable consequences. The next time you are tempted to yield to your old master, remember this: Grace invites you to return and find forgiveness, but it doesn't automatically erase the scars that accompany sin; some could stay with you for life.

In spite of the terrible consequences sins may bring, grace also means we allow others the freedom to choose, regardless. To do otherwise abuses as much as those who use their freedom as a license to sin. I am a firm believer in mutual accountability, but grace means I will not force or manipulate or judge or attempt to control you, nor should you do those things to me. It means we will keep on helping others to freedom by providing breathing holes. It means we deliberately let go so each of us can grow and learn on our own; otherwise, we shall never enjoy the liberty of an open sea. For most of us, letting others go is neither natural nor easy. Because we care, it is more our tendency to give people hints or advice. The thought of letting them fail or fall is extremely painful to us, but God treats us like that virtually every day of our lives. We tend to clutch, not release . . . to put people in our frame and not allow them any breathing holes unless and until they accept the shape of our molds.

🕮 REFLECTING ON GRACE

How can God's grace of giving us freedom to choose be both wonderful and dangerous at the same time?

List three ways you can deliberately let go of someone you've been attempting to control:

1.

2.

3.

Define the difference between mutual accountability and manipulation. In which of your relationships have you experienced each one?

 AWAKENING TO GRACE

John 15:5–14

I am the vine, you are the branches; he who abides in Me and I in him, he bears much fruit, for apart from Me you can do nothing. If anyone does not abide in Me, he is thrown away as a branch and dries up; and they gather them, and cast them into the fire and they are burned. If you abide in Me, and My words abide in you, ask whatever you wish, and it will be done for you. My Father is glorified by this, that you bear much fruit, and so prove to be My disciples. Just as the Father has loved Me, I have also loved you; abide in My love. If you keep My commandments, you will abide in My love; just as I have kept My Father's commandments and abide in His love. These things I have spoken to you so that My joy may be in you, and that your joy may be made full.

This is My commandment, that you love one another, just as I have loved you. Greater love has no one than this, that one lay down his life for his friends. You are My friends if you do what I command you.

According to the passage, how can you abide in Christ's love?

What are the benefits of choosing to obey Christ?

How does Jesus link your personal obedience with an expression of grace toward others?

WALKING IN GRACE

Watching a loved one make mistakes can be devastating. How can you display a caring spirit while still allowing them freedom to choose?

What specific "breathing holes" do you desire in your life? What "breathing holes" have others asked you to give them?

Do you have a specific person you've been afraid to release? Today, pray for strength to relinquish that person to Christ's authority.

Don't you realize that whatever you choose to obey becomes your master?

Romans 6:16 NLT

CAREFUL WARNING TO ALL WHO ARE FREE

*E*ven those who live in a free country need warnings. So we shouldn't be surprised that God gives His own a few warnings lest we abuse our privileges as people under grace. These warnings are set forth in verses 16 through 23 of Romans 6. None of them is complicated, but to grasp each one we'll need to concentrate. For some reason, this information is not commonly heard in many churches today. So we must be taught to handle grace rather carefully. An overall principle is woven into the words of verse 16:

Do you not know that when you present yourselves to someone as slaves for obedience, you are slaves of the one whom you obey, either of sin resulting in death, or of obedience resulting in righteousness?

If you were to ask me to give you in one sentence what the balance of chapter 6 is teaching, it would be this: *How we live depends on the master we choose.* "Do you not know that when you present yourselves to someone as slaves for obedience, you are slaves of the one whom you obey?" Why, of course! Submission to a master is tantamount to slavery to the same master. And what are the alternatives?

There are only two: "either of sin resulting in death, or of obedience resulting in righteousness." Every day we live, we have a choice to do what is right or what is wrong. When we send our young children off to school, we tell them, "Now, sweetheart, you need to know that Mom and Dad won't be there to make your decisions. You will find some kids at school who will encourage you to do what is right, and you'll find others who will lead you to disobey and do what is wrong. Make the right choice. Select your friends carefully. Be smart."

REFLECTING ON GRACE

Recall the last choice you faced that forced you to choose between right and wrong. What process did you go through to make your decision?

What tools does God's grace give you to make right choices in your life?

What does the phrase "slaves to obedience" bring to mind? How do you relate to this term?

 AWAKENING TO GRACE

Galatians 5:16–23

But I say, walk by the Spirit, and you will not carry out the desire of the flesh. For the flesh sets its desire against the Spirit, and the Spirit against the flesh; for these are in opposition to one another, so that you may not do the things that you please. But if you are led by the Spirit, you are not under the Law. Now the deeds of the flesh are evident, which are: immorality, impurity, sensuality, idolatry, sorcery, enmities, strife, jealousy, outbursts of anger, disputes, dissensions, factions, envying, drunkenness, carousing, and things like these, of which I forewarn you just as I have forewarned you, that those who practice such things will not inherit

> *the kingdom of God. But the fruit of the Spirit*
> *is love, joy, peace, patience, kindness, goodness,*
> *faithfulness, gentleness, self-control; against*
> *such things there is no law.*

What does this passage regard as the conflict inherent in every choice you make?

Give specific examples of when your life clearly produced either the fruit of the Holy Spirit or the fruit of your sinful nature.

With which fruit of the Spirit do you struggle the most?

 WALKING IN GRACE

Consider the people you've chosen to surround you. What kinds of choices do they make and encourage you to make?

How does your presence influence the choices of others?

If someone were to look at your life yesterday, last month, or last year, who would your actions reveal your master to be?

DAY 22

You have forgiven the guilt of your people—yes, you have covered all their sins.

Psalm 85:2 NLT

TWO-DIMENSIONAL GRACE

Grace comes to us in two dimensions, vertical and horizontal. Vertical grace centers on our relationship with God. It is amazing. It frees us from the demands and condemnation of the Mosaic Law. It announces hope to the sinner—the gift of eternal life, along with all its benefits.

Horizontal grace centers on our human relationships. It is charming. It frees us from the tyranny of pleasing people and adjusting our lives to the demands and expectations of human opinion. It gives relief—the enjoyment of freedom along with all its benefits. It silences needless guilt and removes self-imposed shame.

Few people realize better than non-Christians how guilt-ridden many Christians are. A lady in our congregation tells of a conversation she had with a fellow student while the two of them were students at the Berkeley campus of the University of California. He knew she was a Christian, and he made it painfully clear that he had no

118

interest whatsoever in her faith. When she asked why, his answer bore the sting of reality: "Because the most guilt-ridden people I know are Christians. No thanks."

This is a good time for me to ask you two probing questions. Only you can answer them:

Do you add to others' guilt or do you lessen it?

Are you the type who promotes another's liberty or restrains it?

Both questions have to do with attitude, don't they? We do what we do with others because of the way we think. Our attitude, therefore, is crucial. It is also at our mercy. We have full control of which attitude we shall have: charming and gracious, or restrictive and rigid. Liberty or legalism will be the result. Depending on our attitude, we are grace givers or grace killers.

✍ REFLECTING ON GRACE

If you admitted that you have added to others' guilt or attempted to restrain their liberty, what have been the key motives behind your actions?

To what extent do you allow your attitudes or feelings to direct your actions? What can you do to make sure your attitude stays at your mercy?

As you read these devotionals, which type of grace—vertical or horizontal—do you find yourself spending most time focusing on? Pray that your relationship with God and others may *both* be flooded with grace.

🐾 AWAKENING TO GRACE

Luke 6:37–42 NIV

"Do not judge, and you will not be judged. Do not condemn, and you will not be condemned. Forgive, and you will be forgiven. Give, and it will be given to you. A good measure, pressed down, shaken together and running over, will be poured into your lap. For with the measure you use, it will be measured to you."

He also told them this parable: "Can a blind man lead a blind man? Will they not both fall into a pit? A student is not above his teacher, but everyone who is fully trained will be like his teacher. Why do you look at the

> *speck of sawdust in your brother's eye and pay no attention to the plank in your own eye? How can you say to your brother, 'Brother, let me take the speck out of your eye,' when you yourself fail to see the plank in your own eye? You hypocrite, first take the plank out of your eye, and then you will see clearly to remove the speck from your brother's eye."*

While speaking to the crowd, what did Jesus reveal as the key to demonstrating a spirit of grace?

According to this passage, what consequences follow maintaining an attitude that adds to someone else's guilt?

How does Jesus' illustration regarding the blind leading the blind relate to someone who judges another?

WALKING IN GRACE

What kind of picture do your words and actions paint about Christianity to nonbelievers? How do you know?

Have you been a grace giver or a grace killer? What is one step you can take to become a grace giver?

*And whatever you do or say, let it be
as a representative of the Lord Jesus,
all the while giving thanks through
him to God the Father.*

Colossians 3:17 NLT

GUIDING GRACE

*I*n his letter to the Romans, Paul goes into great detail
regarding the issue of personal freedom—greater
detail than almost anywhere else in his writings. In the
fourteenth chapter, for example, he sets forth four very
practical guidelines that can be followed by all who are
serious about releasing others in grace. My hope is that we
not only learn what they are but, equally important, that
we spend our days following them.

Guideline 1: *Accepting others is basic to letting them
be.* The problem was not a meat problem, it was a love
problem, an acceptance problem. It still is. How often we
restrict our love by making it conditional: "If you will (or
won't), then I will accept you." Paul starts there: "Accept
one another!" In other words, "Let's allow each other the
freedom to hold to convictions that are unlike our own . . .
and accept them in spite of that difference." Those who

didn't eat (called here "weak in faith") were exhorted to accept and not judge those who ate. And those who ate were exhorted to accept and not regard with contempt those who did not eat. The secret lies in accepting one another. All of this is fairly easy to read so long as I stay on the issue of eating meat. That one is safe because it isn't a current taboo. It's easy to accept those folks today because they don't exist!

Guideline 2: *Refusing to dictate to others allows the Lord freedom to direct their lives.* I especially appreciate the statement at the end of verse 5: "Let each man be fully convinced in his own mind." Give people room to make up their minds. Do you have a few new converts who are a part of your life and ministry? Do you want to help them grow toward maturity? Here is how: Let them grow up differently. Let them learn at their own pace, just like you had to learn, including failures and mistakes. If you really want grace to awaken, be easier on them than others were on you. Don't make up their minds—let them! Don't step in and push your weight around—give them plenty of space. Whatever you do, don't control and manipulate them to get what you want.

Be an accepting model of grace. Refuse all temptations to be a brother hasher or sister smasher. We already have too many of them roaming around the religious landscape. And nothing catches the attention of the unsaved world quicker than those times when we Christians beat up on one another. Don't think the unsaved world doesn't notice our cannibalism.

Guideline 3: *Freeing others means we never assume a position we're not qualified to fill.* This, in one sentence, is enough to stop any person from judging another. We're not qualified. We lack full knowledge. How often we have jumped to wrong conclusions, made judgmental statements, only to find out later how off-base we were—then wished we could cut out our tongue.

Guideline 4: *Loving others requires us to express our liberty wisely.* In other words, love must rule. I'm not my own, I'm bought with a price. My goal is not to please me; it is to please my Lord Jesus, my God. It is not to please you; it is to please my Lord. The same is true for you. So the bottom line is this: I don't adapt my life according to what you may say; I adapt my life according to the basis of my love for you because I answer to Christ. And so do you.

✍ REFLECTING ON GRACE

What godly sounding conditions have you tried to put on others before accepting them as brothers and sisters in Christ?

Which of the author's four guidelines, if followed, would change your relationships with others the most? Why?

Why is it so important to allow new Christians to grow up differently in Christ than you did?

✍ AWAKENING TO GRACE

1 Corinthians 10:25–33

Eat anything that is sold in the meat market without asking questions for conscience' sake; FOR THE EARTH IS THE LORD'S, AND ALL IT CONTAINS. If one of the unbelievers invites you and you want to go, eat anything that is set before you without asking questions for conscience' sake. But if anyone says to you, "This is meat sacrificed to idols," do not eat it, for the sake of

the one who informed you, and for conscience'
sake; I mean not your own conscience, but the
other man's; for why is my freedom judged by
another's conscience? If I partake with thank-
fulness, why am I slandered concerning that for
which I give thanks?

Whether, then, you eat or drink or whatever
you do, do all to the glory of God. Give no
offense either to Jews or to Greeks or to the
church of God; just as I also please all men in
all things, not seeking my own profit but the
profit of the many, so that they may be saved.

What practical guidelines for grace did Paul set up in this
passage?

According to Paul, how should your conscience play a part
in deciding your actions?

In what ways can you—a believer set free in Christ—exemplify grace to nonbelievers?

 WALKING IN GRACE

All Christians are weak in some areas and stronger in others. Honestly identify several weaknesses and strengths in your own life.

Name some close friends who hold different convictions than you do about various *spiritual* matters. How have you maintained a relationship of grace with them in the midst of your differences?

Today, how will you turn your focus away from pleasing others to pleasing the Lord?

Day 24

When I am with those who follow the Jewish laws, I do the same, even though I am not subject to the law, so that I can bring them to Christ.

1 Corinthians 9:20 NLT

A Few Actions That Signify Grace

I want to focus our attention today on the concluding verses in Romans 14. Read verse 19 slowly and thoughtfully. "So then let us pursue the things which make for peace and the building up of one another." On the basis of that great statement, consider the first of four action steps.

1. *Concentrate on things that encourage peace and assist others' growth.* An idea that works for me is to filter whatever I do through a twofold "grid"—two questions that keep me focused: (a) Is this going to make a lot of waves, or will it encourage peace? (b) Is this going to hurt and offend, or will it help and strengthen my brother or sister? Let's commit ourselves anew to encouragement and affirmation.

2. *Remember that sabotaging saints hurts the work of God.* "Don't tear down the work of God for the sake of

food." (v. 20). You sabotage the saints when you flaunt your liberty, knowing that they have convictions against it. That is not fair. Frankly, that is fighting dirty. Scripture calls it "regarding with contempt," and counsels us against it. Enjoy your liberty with discretion.

3.   *Exercise your liberty only with those who can enjoy it with you.* I repeat, that means to keep it private and personal. What others don't know can't hurt them. That's not deception; it's wise and necessary restraint. It isn't prompted by hypocrisy but by love.

4.   *Determine where you stand and refuse to play God in anyone else's life.* That may sound simple and easy, but it is tougher than it may seem. Be absolutely sure you are right, then press on, regardless. By letting others be, you free yourself to give full attention to what God is trying to make of you. You have neither the time nor the energy to keep holding on. Love demands that you let go.

Reflecting on Grace

In your closest relationships, you're probably well versed on the other person's hot buttons. How might you "concentrate on peace" in these friendships?

When confronting legalism, anything you do has the propensity to cause waves. How can you remain spiritually free while exercising self-restraint with certain people?

What other actions would you add to this list as good advice (not strict rules) for balanced, gracious living?

 Awakening to Grace

1 Corinthians 9:19–23 NLT

This means I am not bound to obey people just because they pay me, yet I have become a servant of everyone so that I can bring them to Christ. When I am with the Jews, I become one of them so that I can bring them to Christ. When I am with those who follow the Jewish laws, I do the same, even though I am not subject to the law, so that I can bring them to Christ. When I am with the Gentiles who do not have the Jewish law, I fit in with them as much as I can. In this way, I gain their confidence and bring them to Christ. But I do not discard the law of God; I obey the law of Christ. When I am with those who are oppressed, I

> *share their oppression so that I might bring*
> *them to Christ. Yes, I try to find common*
> *ground with everyone so that I might bring*
> *them to Christ. I do all this to spread the Good*
> *News, and in doing so I enjoy its blessings.*

In these verses, how does Paul illustrate a clear understanding of both his freedom in Christ and the dedication to grace?

What is Paul's ultimate motive in becoming like a Jew or a Gentile?

Where do Paul's personal beliefs intersect with the convictions held by people from different backgrounds?

🖎 WALKING IN GRACE

Regarding the fourth action step, how can you "determine where you stand" in your beliefs?

Sensitivity begins with awareness. Identify people in your life with whom you will be able to exercise more freedom and those with whom you need to be more sensitive.

Choosing never to exercise your freedom, even in private, as some ultracautious gesture toward others, wastes God's beautiful gift of grace! In what particular area do you need to be less self-conscious about exercising your freedom?

*The human body has many parts,
but the many parts make up only one
body. So it is with the body of Christ.*

1 Corinthians 12:12 NLT

Agreeing about Disagreements

*A*s much as we may pursue peace, and as positive and tactful as we may be, there will still be occasions when disagreements arise. As one wag put it, "Life ain't no exact science," which brings me to the first of four facts with which everyone (well, most of us) would agree.

1. *Disagreements are inevitable.* Throughout this book, I have emphasized the value of variety and the importance of individuality. The downside of that is it leaves the door open for differing opinions. I say downside only because those inevitable differences can lead to strong disagreements. There will be opposing viewpoints and a variety of perspectives on most subjects. Tastes differ as well as preferences. That is why they make vanilla and chocolate and strawberry ice cream, why they build Fords and Chevys, Chryslers and Cadillacs, Hondas and Toyotas. That is why our nation has room for Democrats and Republicans, conservatives and liberals — and moder-

ates. The tension is built into our system. It is what freedom is all about, including religious freedom. I am fairly
firm in my theological convictions, but that doesn't mean
you (or anyone) must agree with me. All this explains why
I place so much importance on leaving "wobble room" in
our relationships. One's theological persuasion may not
bend, but one's involvements with others must. Leaders
are especially in need of leaving "wobble room" if they
hope to relieve steam from inevitable tensions.

2. *Even the godly will sometimes disagree.* When I
was younger I had difficulty with this one. I couldn't
understand how two people who loved the Lord with
equal passion and who believed the Bible with equal zeal
could come to different conclusions. In my two-by-four
mind I was convinced that all godly minds held to identi-
cal conclusions. Not so! To my amazement, I soon discov-
ered that there were not only various opinions on the same
subject, but that God had the audacity to bless those who
disagreed with me. I believe it was Dr. Bob Cook, while he
was president of The King's College, who wisely said,
"God reserves the right to use people who disagree with
me." I'll go one step further, for I am now convinced that
God is not nearly so narrow as many of His people are. I
find that God is much easier to live with than most of His
followers . . . far more tolerant, certainly full of more grace
and forgiveness than all of us are.

Unlike us, when He forgives, He forgets the transgression and removes it as far as east is from west. Perhaps you have heard of the man who loved the Lord, but he couldn't seem to conquer a particular sin. Time and again through the week he would come before the Lord and confess the same transgression. In all sincerity, he would tell God how much he hated what he had done and how grateful he was for God's grace in forgiving him. Wouldn't you know it, by Saturday of that same struggling week he was back on his knees: "Here I come again, Lord, with the same sin . . . asking Your forgiveness and claiming Your cleansing." To his surprise, he heard God's audible answer: "What sin?"

There will be no denominations in heaven, no categories of Christians—only the vast company of the saints, and only then will there be perfect harmony of heart and complete unanimity of agreement. Until then, count on it, even the godly will disagree.

3.   *In every disagreement there are the same two ingredients:* (a) an issue and (b) various viewpoints. The issue is usually objective and involves principles. The viewpoints are subjective and involve personalities. And therein lies the sum and substance of a clash, which could be defined as a disagreement over an issue because of opposing points of view. I will be candid with you: Every time I have remembered those two basic ingredients in the midst of a disagreement, I have been able to keep calm and think

clearly. When I have forgotten them, almost without exception I have failed to negotiate my way through the clash with wisdom. Furthermore, I have regretted something I said in the heat of verbal exchange. Those two simple ingredients have never failed to help me keep cool. Why? The next fact will explain.

4.   *In many disagreements each side is valid.* As "liberal" as you may think that sounds, chew on it before you toss it aside. On numerous occasions when I have encountered a brother or sister who felt as strongly as I about the other side of the argument, I came to realize it was not so much an I-am-right-and-you-are-wrong matter as it was an I-see-it-from-his-perspective-and-you-from-that-perspective matter. Both sides of most disagreements have strengths and weaknesses, which means neither side is an airtight slam dunk. Nevertheless, any disagreement can lead to a serious, permanent rift in a relationship . . . and sometimes (this may surprise you) that is God's will. There are times God chooses to spread the good news of His Son rapidly in different directions by having two capable servants of His have a major disagreement. As they separate and minister effectively in two different locations, He accomplishes a greater objective than their being in agreement.

REFLECTING ON GRACE

Consider a time when you experienced a disagreement with a fellow brother or sister in Christ. How did you choose to look at the situation? What were the consequences of that choice?

Whom do you know that God has chosen to use despite (or because of) a disagreement with you?

How can you stand firm in your theological persuasion while maintaining a flexible involvement with others?

 AWAKENING TO GRACE

Acts 15:36–41

And after some days Paul said to Barnabas, "Let us return and visit the brethren in every city in which we proclaimed the word of the Lord, and see how they are." Barnabas wanted to take John, called Mark, along with them also. But Paul kept insisting that they should not take him along who had deserted them in Pamphylia and had not gone with them to the

> *work. And there occurred such a sharp disagreement that they separated from one another, and Barnabas took Mark with him and sailed away to Cyprus. But Paul chose Silas and left, being committed by the brethren to the grace of the Lord. And he was traveling through Syria and Cilicia, strengthening the churches.*

What disagreement is presented in these verses? Who are the major characters involved and what were their positions?

What positive effects on the ministry came from the separation of Paul and Barnabas?

What do you learn from this situation about God's ability to use such disagreements to His glory?

WALKING IN GRACE

Give examples of how you could demonstrate "wobble room" in one of your troubling relationships.

In your next disagreement (and there will be a next one), concentrate on separating the issue from the two or more viewpoints being presented. How might this exercise change your perspective in the disagreement?

What are several benefits of having diverse opinions within the body of Christ? What are some of the challenges? Where does grace fit in?

DAY 26

See that no one pays back evil for evil, but always try to do good to each other and to everyone else.

1 Thessalonians 5:15 NLT

MODELING GRACE THROUGH DISAGREEABLE TIMES

Let me offer several comments that may help you handle future disagreeable times in a gracious manner.

First, *always leave room for an opposing viewpoint.* If you don't have room for an opposing viewpoint, you're not going to do well when you get teenagers. Teens can be among our best teachers. I know ours have been. They haven't always been right, nor have I. However, I have learned in rearing teenagers that they are great at pointing out another point of view, if nothing else than just to make me think, just to challenge me, just to remind me that there is another way of viewing things. I can assure you, it has helped me in my ministry. It has certainly helped me in my relationship with those to whom I am personally accountable. Opposition is good for our humility.

Second, *if an argument must occur, don't assassinate.*

141

An argument—even a strong clash—is one thing, but killing folks is another. I have seen individuals in an argument verbally hit below the belt and assault another's character. I've seen a lot of mud slinging happen in arguments related to the work of the church. I've seen brutal character assassinations occur in the name of religion—in public speaking as well as in writing—and they are all ugly memories. No need for that. If we must fight, let's fight fair.

Third, *if you don't get your way, get over it; get on with life.* If you don't get your way in a vote at a church, get over it. The vote was taken (if the church has integrity, the vote was handled with fairness), now get on with it. Just press on. And don't rehearse the fight or the vote year after year. The work of God slows down when we are not big enough to take it on the chin and say, "We lost!" Having been raised in the South, I didn't know the South lost the Civil War until I was in junior high school . . . and even then it was debatable among my teachers. Be big enough to say, "We lost." Grace will help.

Fourth, *sometimes the best solution is a separation.* There is good biblical support for this, remember. Paul and Barnabas simply couldn't go on together, so they separated. If I can't go on with the way things are in a particular ministry, I need to resign! But in doing so I should not drag people through my unresolved conflicts because I didn't get my way. If separation is the best solution, doing it graciously is essential. If your disagreements are starting to outweigh your agreements, you ought to give strong consideration to pulling out. Who knows? This may be God's way of moving you on to another dimension of ministry.

Reflecting on Grace

What is your response when mud slinging takes place in your presence? How can you respond graciously yet firmly?

Sadly, many times separation in ministry is often the *first* solution instead of the last. What can you do to encourage unity and grace in your ministry?

Name the last time you allowed an opposing viewpoint to teach you humility.

 AWAKENING TO GRACE

1 Corinthians 6:1–8

Does any one of you, when he has a case against his neighbor, dare to go to law before the unrighteous and not before the saints? Or do you not know that the saints will judge the world? If the world is judged by you, are you not competent to constitute the smallest law courts? Do you not know that we will judge angels? How much more matters of this life? So if you have law courts dealing with matters of this life, do you appoint them as judges who are of no account in the church? I say this to your shame. Is it so, that there is not among you one wise man who will be able to decide between his brethren, but brother goes to law with brother, and that before unbelievers? Actually, then, it is already a defeat for you, that you have lawsuits with one another. Why not rather be wronged? Why not rather be defrauded? On the contrary, you yourselves wrong and defraud. You do this even to your brethren.

What was Paul's advice to believers for handling disagreements in the early church?

According to Paul, what would be the result if believers resolved their disagreements as unbelievers do?

Paul's closing advice to let yourself be wronged sounds unfair and out of place in today's world. What spiritual and mental benefits could be gained from following this suggestion?

 ## WALKING IN GRACE

Today, do your best to listen to an opposing viewpoint. What would it mean to let someone win an argument or disagreement in order to save the friendship?

Gracious separation in ministry is not the same as separation in marriage. If you've experienced more disagreements than agreements with your spouse, what can you do to work toward graceful resolution while keeping your marriage strong?

What argument have you been holding on to because you didn't get your way? Will you let it go today in prayer?

For I am confident of this very thing, that He who began a good work in you will perfect it until the day of Christ Jesus.

Philippians 1:6

AWAKENING GRACE

Want a boost of encouragement? Our God is working toward that end in all of His children. It is His constant pursuit, His daily agenda, as He points us toward our final destination, "the Celestial City," as Bunyan calls it. Having cleansed our hearts of the debris of inward corruptions and the dust of sin's domination, God is now daily at work awakening grace within us, perfecting our character and bringing it to completion.

As I think about our becoming people of awakening grace, I believe at least three things are involved in the process:

First, it *takes time*. Learning anything takes time. Becoming good models of grace, it seems, takes years! Like wisdom, it comes slowly. But God is in no hurry as He purges graceless characteristics from us. But we can count on this, for sure: He is persistent.

Second, it *requires pain*. The "dust" in our room doesn't settle easily. I know of no one who has adopted a "grace state of mind" painlessly. Hurt is part of the curriculum in God's schoolroom.

Third, it *means change*. Being "graceless" by nature, we find it difficult to be anything different. We lack it, we resist it, we fail to show it, but God never stops His relentless working. He is committed to our becoming more like His Son. Remember? "He who began a good work . . . *will* carry it on to completion" (NIV).

❧ REFLECTING ON GRACE

What recurring trial in your life might actually be part of God's curriculum as He teaches you grace over time?

What pain have you seen or experienced as a result of a specific gracious act that you did? How might you relate that pain to Christ's pain on the cross?

Compare your life now with how you were five years ago. In what ways has God continued His work of grace in you?

 AWAKENING TO GRACE

Romans 8:28–29

And we know that God causes all things to work together for good to those who love God, to those who are called according to His purpose. For those whom He foreknew, He also predestined to become conformed to the image of His Son, so that He might be the firstborn among many brethren.

How does this passage confirm that grace awakening is a process that involves time, pain, and change?

According to the passage, how can you reconcile your painful struggles in life to God's grace?

What does it mean to you that you have been "predestined to become conformed to the image" of Christ?

WALKING IN GRACE

Reflect upon the three areas involved in becoming a person of awakening grace. After each, record personal experiences that God has used to teach you about each one.

Grace takes time:

Grace requires pain:

Grace means change:

Describe a specific time this past week when you saw God at work in your daily life to promote gracious living.

Imagine that God's good work in you has been fully completed. What things have changed in your life? Choose one insight to pray about today.

DAY 28

He has removed our rebellious acts as far away from us as the east is from the west.

Psalm 103:12 NLT

GRACE THAT RELEASES

One characteristic of a grace awakening ministry deserves special attention: *release from past failures.* A ministry of grace doesn't keep bringing up the past for the purpose of holding it over people. There is an absence of shame. Paul addresses this in 1 Timothy 1:12–14:

I thank Christ Jesus our Lord, who has strengthened me, because He considered me faithful, putting me into service, even though I was formerly a blasphemer and a persecutor and a violent aggressor. Yet I was shown mercy because I acted ignorantly in unbelief; and the grace of our Lord was more than abundant, with the faith and love which are found in Christ Jesus.

You may be surprised to know that the apostle Paul had every reason to feel ashamed. He was one whose past was dreadful: "formerly a blasphemer . . . persecutor . . . violent aggressor." Then how could the same man write, "I am not ashamed" (2 Timothy 1:12)? He gives us the answer here in 1 Timothy 1:14: Grace was more than abundant. Blasphemy had abounded in his past, but grace superabounded. Violence and brutality had abounded, but grace superabounded.

What if it read "divorcee"? What if it read "homosexual"? What if it read "addict"? I realize it reads "blasphemer, persecutor, aggressor." But what if it read "prostitute" or "ex-con" or "financial failure" or "murderer"? In a grace-awakened ministry, none of those things in the past are allowed to hold those people in bondage. They are released, forgiven, and the believer is allowed to go on to a new life in Christ.

Grace releases people, not only from sin but from shame. Do you do that in your ministry? Or do you make a note of those things and keep reminding yourself when that particular name comes up: "Well, you know, you'd better watch her" or, "You've gotta watch him." Do you give people reasons to feel greater shame? Who knows what battles of shame most folks struggle with? It is enormous.

REFLECTING ON GRACE

Paul acknowledged his past failings without allowing them to bring him back under the control of guilt. How well have you been able to do that? Why?

How close do you come to Paul's example of separating humility and shame?

What sins abound today that are commonly regarded as difficult for God to erase? In what ways has your ministry combated this assumption?

 AWAKENING TO GRACE

Hebrews 4:13–16

And there is no creature hidden from His sight, but all things are open and laid bare to the eyes of Him with whom we have to do.

Therefore since then we have a great high priest who has passed through the heavens, Jesus the Son of God, let us hold fast our confession. For we do not have a high priest who cannot sympathize with our weaknesses, but

One who has been tempted in all things as we are, yet without sin. Therefore let us draw near with confidence to the throne of grace, so that we may receive mercy and find grace to help in time of need.

How do these verses display a balance between God's sovereignty regarding your sin and God's grace in His relationship with you?

Through whom does God enact His grace toward humanity?

How does Jesus model a spirit of total acceptance and understanding of personal weakness?

🖎 WALKING IN GRACE

Describe a time in your ministry when grace abounded. What specifically led to such gracious gestures?

Have you ever warned others about a specific individual's past sins? How can you be an example of someone who truly wipes the slate clean?

Be someone who people can depend on for unconditional love and grace! Start building this reputation today by releasing someone in his or her walk with Christ. Who will be the first beneficiary of your desire to practice grace?

DAY 29

So again I say, each man must love his wife as he loves himself, and the wife must respect her husband.

Ephesians 5:33 NLT

MARITAL GRACE

*T*he more the grace of God is awakened in a marriage, the less husbands will attempt to control and restrict and the less wives will feel the need to "please no matter what." It makes marriage easier to manage.

Grace releases and affirms. It doesn't smother.

Grace values the dignity of individuals. It doesn't destroy.

Grace supports and encourages. It isn't jealous or suspicious.

I know whereof I speak. For more years than I care to remember, I was consumed with jealousy. I was so insecure and fearful it wasn't uncommon for me to drill Cynthia with questions—petty, probing questions that were little more than veiled accusations. It is amazing she endured it. Finally, we had one of those famous showdown confrontations every married couple has had. No need to repeat it, but she made it painfully clear that I was smothering her; I was imagining things she never even thought of doing . . . and it had to stop. Her words hurt, but she did the right thing. I took her seriously.

I went to work on this ugly side of my life. I confessed my jealousy to Cynthia. I assured her I would never again treat her with such a lack of trust. I asked God for grace to help, for relief from the destructive habit I had formed, for the ability to love and give myself to this woman without all the choking conditions. I distinctly recall how much an understanding of grace helped. It was as if grace were finally "awake" in my life, and I could appropriate its power for the first time. It seemed to free me, first in small ways, and finally in major areas. I can honestly say today that I do not entertain a single jealous thought. Grace *literally* wiped the slate clean.

REFLECTING ON GRACE

How does the awakening of grace assist in balancing a marriage?

Consider what each of the following promises means for your marriage.

Grace releases and affirms my spouse.

Grace values the dignity of my spouse.

Grace supports and encourages my spouse.

Which of the above concepts is most difficult for you right now? Explain.

 AWAKENING TO GRACE

Ruth 3:1–11

Then Naomi her mother-in-law said to her, "My daughter, shall I not seek security for you, that it may be well with you? Now is not Boaz our kinsman, with whose maids you were? Behold, he winnows barley at the threshing floor tonight. Wash yourself therefore, and anoint yourself and put on your best clothes, and go down to the threshing floor; but do not make yourself known to the man until he has finished eating and drinking. It shall be when he lies down, that you shall notice the place where he lies, and you shall go and uncover his feet and lie down; then he will tell you what you shall do." She said to her, "All that you say I will do."

So she went down to the threshing floor and did according to all that her mother-in-law had commanded her. When Boaz had eaten and drunk and his heart was merry, he went to lie down at the end of the heap of grain; and she came secretly, and uncovered his feet and lay down. It happened in the middle of the night that the man was startled and bent forward; and behold, a woman was lying at his feet. He said, "Who are you?" And she answered, "I am Ruth your maid. So spread your covering over your maid, for you are a close relative." Then he said, "May you be blessed of the LORD, my daughter. You have shown your last kindness to be better than the first by not going after young men, whether poor or rich. Now, my daughter, do not fear. I will do for you whatever you ask,

for all my people in the city know that you are
a woman of excellence."

How did Ruth display an attitude of trust in her relationship with her mother-in-law?

In what ways did Boaz show Ruth grace in her vulnerable
state?

What resulted from Boaz's grace toward Ruth?

❧ WALKING IN GRACE

Recall a confrontation in your marriage that caused you to
reassess your feelings toward your spouse. Was that conflict resolved in a deeper understanding of grace? Why or
why not?

What areas of your marriage could benefit most from an
attitude of grace on your part?

How far are you willing to go in order to secure grace in your marriage? What steps can you take to start this process?

DAY 30

God loves the person who gives cheer-fully.

2 Corinthians 9:7 NLT

THE ATTRACTION OF GRACIOUS GIVING

When I consider the magnetic effects of gracious giving, four qualities immediately emerge. First, grace is so attractive: *Grace individualizes the gift.* When you give by grace, you give individually. You give proportionately to your own income. You have needs and you have an income to meet those needs. That combination is unlike anyone else's on earth. You are an individual. When you give on that basis, your gift is an individual kind of *gift.* We are not all shoved into a tank, blended together, then "required" to give exactly 50 percent. (Though if everyone gave 50 percent, we would have such an enormous surplus in God's work we would not know what to do with the extra . . . but I'm sure we'd quickly find out.) It is much more individualized than that. Grace, remember, brings variety and spontaneity.

Here's the second reason grace is so attractive: *Grace makes the action joyfully spontaneous.* "Not grudgingly or

163

under compulsion, for God loves a cheerful giver" (2 Corinthians 9:7). I never have been able to understand why everyone in the church looks so serious during the offering. Wouldn't it be great if when the offering plates are passed in church next Sunday that instead of grim looks, stoic silence, and soft organ music you heard laughter? I can just imagine: "Can you believe we're doing this?" "Put it in the plate, honey. Isn't this great? Put it in!" . . . followed by little ripples of laughter and applause across the place of worship. Wonderful! Why not? Deep within the heart there is an absence of any compulsion, only spontaneous laughter. The word *cheerful* is literally a Greek term from which we get the word "hilarious." "God loves a *hilarious* giver."

Now for a third reason grace is so attractive: *Grace enables us to link up with God's supply line.* Look at verse 8 of 2 Corinthians 9: "And God is able to make all grace abound to you, that always having all sufficiency in everything, you may have an abundance for every good deed." When we possess an attitude of grace, we give. We give ourselves. We give from what we earn. And He, in turn, gives back in various ways, not matching gift for gift, but in an abundance of ways, He goes beyond.

Fourth: *Grace leads to incomparable results.* "Because of the proof given by this ministry, they will glorify God for your obedience to your confession of the gospel of Christ and for the liberality of your contribution to them and to all, while they also, by prayer on your behalf, yearn for you because of the surpassing grace of God in you" (2 Corinthians 9:13–14).

 REFLECTING ON GRACE

Describe a specific time when an act of giving to others produced an abundance of well-being in your own life.

Besides money, with what has God gifted you that you can use to bless others?

How might the idea of being a "hilarious giver" change the way you give?

 AWAKENING TO GRACE

2 Corinthians 8:12–15 NIV

For if the willingness is there, the gift is acceptable according to what one has, not according to what he does not have. Our desire is not that others might be relieved while you are hard

> *pressed, but that there might be equality. At the present time your plenty will supply what they need, so that in turn their plenty will supply what you need. Then there will be equality, as it is written: "He who gathered much did not have too much, and he who gathered little did not have too little."*

According to the passage, where should you begin when you want to give?

How did God set up a system of balance in giving?

What did Paul point out as one of the most important aspects to remember in giving?

❧ WALKING IN GRACE

Take a moment to consider the manner and amount you give to the Lord. Are there certain aspects of your life that you've refused to share?

In what other ways is your giving individualized and unique in the family of God?

What places in your church or community need a gift that you are able to supply? If you can't think of one, start asking people about their needs and what you can do to help meet them.

CONCLUDING DAY

 Sin is no longer your master, for you are no longer subject to the law, which enslaves you to sin. Instead, you are free by God's grace.

Romans 6:14 NLT

FREE INDEED

*M*y hope has been to create an appetite for grace that is so strong nothing will restrain us from pursuing the freedom and spontaneity it can bring—a longing so deep that a new spiritual dawn, a "grace awakening," if you will, cannot help but burst through the wall of legalism. Since I am a Christian minister, much of my involvement and exposure is in the realm of the church and Christian organizations. It has been my observation that even here most folks are not free; they have not learned to accept and enjoy the grace that has come to us in Jesus Christ. Though He came to set us free, it saddens me to say that many still live behind the wall of bondage. Regrettably, the stones of constraint are everywhere to be found. Instead of being places of enthusiastic, spontaneous worship, many churches and Christian ministries have become institutions that maintain a system of reli-

168

gion with hired officials to guard the gates and to enforce the rules.

In vain I have searched the Bible, looking for examples of early Christians whose lives were marked by rigidity, predictability, inhibition, dullness, and caution. Fortunately, grim, frowning, joyless saints in Scripture are conspicuous by their absence. Instead, the examples I find are of adventurous, risk-taking, enthusiastic, and authentic believers whose joy was contagious even in times of painful trial. Their vision was broad even when death drew near. Rules were few and changes were welcome. The contrast between then and now is staggering.

The difference, I am convinced, is grace. Grace scales the wall and refuses to be restricted. It lives above the demands of human opinion and breaks free from legalistic regulations. Grace dares us to take hold of the sledge of courage and break through longstanding stones. Grace invites us to chart new courses and explore ever-expanding regions, all the while delighting in the unexpected. While others care more about maintaining the wall and fearing those who guard it, grace is constantly looking for ways to freedom. Grace wants faith to fly, regardless of what grim-faced officials may say or think or do.

There is a "grace awakening" loose in the land. Will you become a part of it? While you take your turn with the sledgehammer and pound away, a host of us are standing near, and some of us may be half a world away, cheering you on. Don't think of it as a lonesome, isolated task. You are breaking through to freedom, and no one is more delighted than the Lord Jesus Christ, who has promised you His grace. Never forget His words: "If therefore the Son shall make you free, you shall be free indeed." Stay at it. By the grace of Almighty God, the new movement will someday sweep across every continent and the longstanding wall that has kept people in bondage for centuries will come tumbling down. And we shall all, at last, be free indeed.

REFLECTING ON GRACE

How will you continue to fuel your appetite for grace after you put this book down?

What longstanding stones still need to be broken in your life and ministry?

When legalism creeps in, what will be your strategy for retaining Christ's promise of true and lasting freedom?

 AWAKENING TO GRACE

Colossians 2:13–23 NLT

You were dead because of your sins and because your sinful nature was not yet cut away. Then God made you alive with Christ. He forgave all our sins. He canceled the record that contained the charges against us. He took it and destroyed it by nailing it to Christ's cross. In this way, God disarmed the evil rulers and authorities. He shamed them publicly by his victory over them on the cross of Christ.

So don't let anyone condemn you for what you eat or drink, or for not celebrating certain holy days or new-moon ceremonies or Sabbaths. For these rules were only shadows of the real thing, Christ himself. Don't let anyone condemn you by insisting on self-denial. And don't let anyone say you must worship angels, even though they say they have had visions about this. These people claim to be so humble, but their sinful minds have made them proud. But they are not connected to Christ, the head of the body. For we are joined together in his body by his strong sinews, and we grow only as we get our nourishment and strength from God.

You have died with Christ, and he has set you free from the evil powers of this world. So why do you keep on following rules of the world, such as, "Don't handle, don't eat, don't touch." Such rules are mere human teaching about things that are gone as soon as we use them. These rules may seem wise because they require strong devotion, humility, and severe bodily discipline. But they have no effect when it comes to conquering a person's evil thoughts and desires.

According to the passage, what are several things you are no longer condemned for now that you are alive with Christ?

What does Paul say is the relationship between rules and Christ?

In these verses, what real power does obeying rules have in becoming godly?

🕮 WALKING IN GRACE

Which believers in the Bible do you most identify as "adventurous, risk-taking, enthusiastic, and authentic"? How could you use their lives as a model for your own grace awakening?

Name one thing you can do to make your church a more welcoming atmosphere of grace.

Take time to pray for a real grace awakening in your family, your church, and yourself. In all your relationships, be an instrument of grace today!